Praise for *Opp*

This is an incredibly important boo[...] you've been taught about the impor[...] [...] wants you to forget for a moment all of the tedious and all-consuming planning that leadership gurus want you to do, and cut yourself loose to see and embrace the opportunities right in front of you. It has been said that sometimes "we can't see the forest for the trees"—but it is also true that sometimes we can't see the most important "trees" because we are obsessed by the forest. As the CEO of multiple organizations over my career, I can tell you that virtually all of my "breakthrough moments" had little to do with strategic planning and everything to do with looking, listening, and being available to the opportunities God had placed right in front of me. Do yourself a favor and read *Opportunity Leadership*.

RICHARD STEARNS
President Emeritus, World Vision US; author of *Lead Like It Matters to God*
and *The Hole in Our Gospel*

During my time at Krispy Kreme, I would have loved having Dr. Parrott's *Opportunity Leadership* as a guidebook for our 2008–2016 corporate turnaround. We did not have the luxury of developing five-year plans . . . in the words of Dr. Parrott, we attempted to lead by "*capturing opportunities* rather than *building plans*." To echo Dr. Parrott's theme in this must-read book, I learned the following: If we bury our heads in planning, we are likely to miss the greatest of God's opportunities! At last, someone has written a leadership book for both today and tomorrow!

JIM MORGAN
Former President, Krispy Kreme

Leaders must get out front and make decisions—especially during times of crisis, opportunity, challenge, or danger. Our decisions won't always be right because we face forces beyond our control, but the most effective leaders don't slow down or retreat. Instead, they learn to make adjustments without losing momentum. I've watched Roger lead Belhaven University with courage and decisiveness, and I am thankful he's written a guide for others to follow through the storms of leadership.

HALEY BARBOUR
Governor of Mississippi, 2004–2012

This book is directing you to a level of inspirational leadership that you didn't expect was possible. Incarnational thinking is coming to the end of what you know about something, and you receive the light of the knowledge of God to solve the problem. This book is adding a major leadership principle to our vision. I'm so thankful and encouraged by my dear friend Roger, and his book is something we need to listen to—this book is timely.

JOHN PERKINS
Author of *Let Justice Roll Down* and *He Calls Me Friend*

Opportunity Leadership is an exciting, paradigm-shifting book. It takes everything you ever learned in business school and turns it upside down. Kingdom work takes not only leadership acumen but the courage and faith to follow where God leads. Roger Parrott's ability to inspire you, challenge you, and train you in a new way of thinking will impact your ministry and those you lead for years to come.

SHAUNTI FELDHAHN
Social researcher; author of *For Women Only* and *The Kindness Challenge*

Roger Parrott is one of the most impressive leaders I've ever met. And now he shares his unconventional insights to provide all of us a guide to be more impactful leaders for the kingdom. "The plan is that there is no plan" is not just a provocative philosophy, but Roger shows how he created one of the most innovative universities in the country with this approach. Read this important book and let the tailwinds of God's sovereignty power your leadership strategy.

MICHAEL MOE
Global Silicon Valley Founder/CEO; author of *The Mission Corporation*

God can accomplish more in a short time than we can otherwise plan and implement over many years. I learned that from Bill Bright and have personally experienced it for decades. Roger Parrott has refined and led by that principle for during his many years as president of Belhaven University, and the results are stunning. In *Opportunity Leadership*, he challenges us to recognize and redeem the special opportunities God has prepared in advance for us to do (Eph. 2:10; 5:15–16).

STEVE DOUGLASS
President Emeritus, Cru

Leadership is an art form that requires—especially in recent times full of disruptions—imagination, risk-taking, and intuition, to be guided toward enduring fruitfulness. Dr. Roger Parrott's leadership vision has helped me to steward my giftings as an artist and a leader. Now we are fortunate to have his wisdom written on these pages as a guide to many perplexed by the complexity and fluidity of our times. This book about effective leadership in education and in business now resonates with an artist's journey toward Making.

MAKOTO FUJIMURA
Artist; author of *Art + Faith: A Theology of Making*

With the speed of change, the days of crafting long-term strategic plans are rapidly evaporating. Leaders today have to remain nimble as navigating the unexpected is the new normal. *Opportunity Leadership* challenges leaders to abandon traditional planning practices to become leaders who seek God and are responsive to what He is directing and doing. If you need a breakthrough in your thinking, then this book is for you!

TAMI HEIM
President and CEO, Christian Leadership Alliance

Working closely with him for thirty-five years, I have seen over and over that Roger Parrott believes what he teaches: *God provides us with opportunity after opportunity—beyond our plans.* He has lived this model of leadership—praying, trusting, and working hard in anticipation of God bringing opportunities. In this challenging book, you will gain a renewed call to trust God with your future!

LEIGHTON FORD
Author of *Transforming Leadership*

Opportunity Leadership is a must read for every leader! As someone who plans every waking minute of my day, I'll admit I was a little skeptical of Dr. Parrott's premise that we need to stop planning. But what Dr. Parrott provides is not another planning strategy repackaged, but rather a way of thinking and behaving as a leader. This book provides a guide for leading with clarity, especially when a long-range vision is unclear. It's a mix of self-leadership, emotional intelligence, and values-based leadership that will be a refreshing read for every leader who has been exhausted by the demands of leadership.

JENNI CATRON
Founder of The 4Sight Group; author of *The Four Dimensions of Extraordinary Leadership*

Dr. Roger Parrott exhorts leaders to let go of the perceived control in our planning activities and instructs us in how to step out in faith, trusting that God can *and will* lead us as we watch for the opportunities around us.

PAUL WHITE
Author of 5 *Languages of Appreciation in the Workplace*

Most leadership books are simply new ways of saying what has been said a hundred times before. *Opportunity Leadership* is an exception to that rule. The management philosophy Dr. Parrott advocates in this book is radically different from what most leaders are used to. The uniqueness of this message coupled with Dr. Parrott's extraordinary results demand the attention of every Christian leader.

JORDAN RAYNOR
Executive Chairman of Threshold 360; author of *Redeeming Your Time*

Vince Lombardi once said, "Leaders are made, they are not born." I've had the chance to meet many leaders in my life, but Dr. Roger Parrott is one of the few "leader-makers." His new book, *Opportunity Leadership*, is a MUST READ for all who aspire to leadership and will be a gift to all who take it to heart.

BILLY KIM
Chairman, Far East Broadcasting Company – Korea

Most Christian leadership books advocate corporate business approaches to inform and drive the process. They urge me to seize control of the future with bold plans and persuade staff and stakeholders to follow my lead. Very few urge me to trust God. Instead of being invigorated by the journey, I often just feel weary. *Opportunity Leadership* is different—Dr.. Parrott urges relinquishing control to discover the liberation of letting God take the lead, and watching Him work! I urge my colleagues in ministry leadership to unfurl the sails and embark on this journey with me! Read this book. And do it!

BOB DUKES
President, Worldwide Discipleship Association

As someone who has studied leadership and been around some of the best leaders in sports, Dr. Parrott is the definition of a great leader. From starting a college football program from scratch to writing this amazing book, his voice is an important one for anyone who is looking to lead like Jesus. Go read this book now!

JASON ROMANO
Host of the *Sports Spectrum Podcast*; author *The Uniform of Leadership*

Another leadership book? Not exactly. What Roger Parrot has done, through reflecting on his own experience of faithfully discerning which doors to open and walk through when God knocks with an opportunity, is offer us new language for how many of us lead and a master class in anticipating with joy the unexpected. *Opportunity Leadership* embraces the truth that we are called to walk by faith and lead by faith, yoked to Christ, trusting God, and setting aside our own strategic plans to labor in advancing God's kingdom purposes always and in all ways. We recognize the fluidity and challenge of leading into a future of unchartered cultural territory. If you're ready, Roger Parrott will help you get set and go.

CARMEN LABERGE
Radio host; author of *Speak the Truth: Bring God Back into the Conversation*

Not only can I attest to the principles that Roger lays out for being ready for and responsive to God-given opportunities, I am also thankful for Roger playing a key part in that journey for me personally and with the Lausanne Movement. Leaders, young and old, will be blessed to take this teaching to heart. It is rooted in Scripture and proven experience.

MICHAEL OH
CEO, Lausanne Movement

If you serve God and want to level-up your leadership planning into bigger opportunities, you immediately should read *Opportunity Leadership*. This is a refreshingly open and heart-driven book packed with so many great pieces of wisdom. Thanks for the inspiration, Roger! Looking forward to reading your next one! No pressure! BOOM!

SANGRAM VAJRE
Cofounder and Chief Evangelist of Terminus; *Wall Street Journal* bestselling author of *MOVE*

Opportunity Leadership

STOP PLANNING and
START GETTING RESULTS

ROGER PARROTT

Moody Publishers
CHICAGO

© 2022 by
ROGER PARROTT

Unless otherwise indicated, all Scripture quotations are taken from the Holy Bible, New Living Translation, copyright © 1996, 2004, 2015 by Tyndale House Foundation. Used by permission of Tyndale House Publishers, Carol Stream, Illinois 60188. All rights reserved.

Scripture quotations marked ESV are from the ESV® Bible (The Holy Bible, English Standard Version®), copyright © 2001 by Crossway, a publishing ministry of Good News Publishers. Used by permission. All rights reserved.

Scripture quotations marked NIV are taken from the Holy Bible, New International Version®, NIV®. Copyright © 1973, 1978, 1984, 2011 by Biblica, Inc.™ Used by permission of Zondervan. All rights reserved worldwide. www.zondervan.com The "NIV" and "New International Version" are trademarks registered in the United States Patent and Trademark Office by Biblica, Inc.™

Scripture quotations marked MSG are taken from THE MESSAGE, copyright © 1993, 2002, 2018 by Eugene H. Peterson. Used by permission of NavPress, represented by Tyndale House Publishers. All rights reserved.

Names and details of some stories have been changed to protect the privacy of individuals.

Edited by Ashleigh Slater
Interior design: Ragont Design
Cover design: Studio Gearbox
Cover image of paper boats copyright © 2020 by your / Shutterstock (501987826). All rights reserved.
Cover image of water trail copyright © 2020 by 977_ReX_977 / Shutterstock (1673630698). All rights reserved.

All websites listed herein are accurate at the time of publication but may change in the future or cease to exist. The listing of website references and resources does not imply publisher endorsement of the site's entire contents. Groups and organizations are listed for informational purposes, and listing does not imply publisher endorsement of their activities.

Library of Congress Cataloging-in-Publication Data

Names: Parrott, Roger, author.
Title: Opportunity leadership : stop planning and start getting results /
   Roger Parrott, Ph.D.
Description: Chicago : Moody Publishers, [2022] | Includes bibliographical
   references. | Summary: "No more long-term planning. Instead of
   forecasting and managing the future, opportunity leaders lean into
   God's promptings to capture change—rather than create it.
   Opportunity Leadership shows you how to respond with expediency,
   adeptness, and energy—and discover powerful results like never
   before"-- Provided by publisher.
Identifiers: LCCN 2021043742 (print) | LCCN 2021043743 (ebook) | ISBN
   9780802423214 (paperback) | ISBN 9780802499530 (ebook)
Subjects: LCSH: Leadership--Religious aspects--Christianity. | Christian
   leadership. | Change--Religious aspects--Christianity. | Planning. |
   Opportunity. | BISAC: RELIGION / Christian Living / Leadership &
   Mentoring | BUSINESS & ECONOMICS / Leadership
Classification: LCC BV4597.53.L43 P36 2022 (print) | LCC BV4597.53.L43
   (ebook) | DDC 253--dc23
LC record available at https://lccn.loc.gov/2021043742
LC ebook record available at https://lccn.loc.gov/2021043743

Originally delivered by fleets of horse-drawn wagons, the affordable paperbacks from D. L. Moody's publishing house resourced the church and served everyday people. Now, after more than 125 years of publishing and ministry, Moody Publishers' mission remains the same—even if our delivery systems have changed a bit. For more information on other books (and resources) created from a biblical perspective, go to www.moodypublishers.com or write to:

Moody Publishers
820 N. LaSalle Boulevard
Chicago, IL 60610

1 3 5 7 9 10 8 6 4 2

Printed in the United States of America

To MaryLou

The wind of God has graced us with opportunities
far beyond our wildest dreams.
Inseparably, we have sailed unknown waters with confidence
in God's direction and protection.

You are the billowing mainsail that makes our adventures fulfilling,
the weighted ballast that holds us steady in storms,
the mission-guided compass that assures our course never wavers,
and the cherished treasure that ladens our voyage with joy.

The greatest opportunity God ever gave me
was to marry you and sail life together.
Everything else is inextricably anchored to that gift.
Without you, the rest of the story would never have been written
because I'd have been marooned alone on a sandbar.

Contents

Acknowledgments

Have you noticed nearly all leadership books are written by retired leaders, academicians, speakers, or consultants? Those of us active in leadership don't write because the bar of accountability is set to the highest standard for living out in practice what we encourage for others.

I wrote a leadership book fifteen years ago that pulled back the curtain on my priorities and practices, and I assumed that volume was enough. I never planned to write another leadership book. But God had a different perspective and brought this book about by way of an unexpected opportunity.

Rushing late to our chapel, my assistant hadn't provided me with the typical background summary of the speaker because the provost had planned the service. He had invited an author, Amy Simpson, to help our campus embrace the church's responsibility in addressing mental health lovingly and gracefully.

Over coffee between services, I surprisingly discovered our guest author was also a book acquisition editor for Moody Publishers. Being polite to a harried university president, Amy asked if I was interested in writing a book. I made it clear that I'd already done that, and I just didn't have time to take on a new project.

Pushing a bit further, she asked, "If you were to consider writing, what is most important in leadership?" The next ten minutes spilled out a monologue of passionate advocacy for what I would come to call

Opportunity Leadership. Although cut off mid-diatribe because the next service was starting, I clarified that I didn't want to write. Amy didn't let it go and followed up a few days later with an email, then a few phone calls, and eventually a consultation that led to this book.

I'm thankful to Amy Simpson for her persistence in initiating this work and then helping to shape the ideas, priorities, and message of *Opportunity Leadership*. I appreciate the accommodating and nurturing culture of Moody Publishers, who have made this process invigorating, including Jeremy Slager, Manager of Book Marketing, and Drew Dyck, who took over the editing responsibility from Amy just as the manuscript was finalized.

I'm especially thankful for the talent of Ashleigh Slater, developmental editor, who has strengthened the manuscript to ensure it carries the intended message. She is marvelous.

Most importantly, the insights shared in *Opportunity Leadership* are due to the gift of a marvelous university that has stretched, pulled, grown, and adjusted as we've learned to abandon traditional planning to find God's best future. I have been blessed:

- Our board of trustees has been steadfast in their support and trust through nearly three decades of ministry together. I'm forever indebted to the four chairs of the board who have been crucial partners during differing strategic seasons: Stuart Irby, Charles Cannada, Cal Wells, and Jimmy Hood.

- Our faculty are out of the ordinary in their willingness to cast off traditional structures of higher education to find God's higher calling. Without their godly spirit of service, the university would never have the chance to seek opportunities rather than depend on traditional planning.

- The administrative staff is the front line of Opportunity Leadership as the university walks through open doors. They are always responsive to doing things differently, faster, and bigger than we expected. They have repeatedly proven they can do what many assume is impossible.

- Our vice presidents, who work closest with me every day, are a group of top-flight professionals who think aggressively, envision imaginatively, and execute exceptionally. Especially during our latest intense season of opportunities, their teamwork and friendship mean the world to me. I am deeply grateful for the joy of working with Brad Smith, Audrey Kelleher, Kevin Russell, Scott Little, Jeff Rickels, David Tarrant, and David Potvin.

I am honored that God has allowed me to join with these colleagues in this remarkable metamorphosis to cast off traditional planning and become utterly dependent on God for the future.

Many say that leadership is a lonely responsibility. I couldn't disagree more. But writing a book is truly a lonely task, although thankfully, I didn't have to do it alone.

This work would never have been possible without the wisdom, iron-sharpening-iron exchanges, wordsmithing, candid critiques, and endless discussions with my wife, MaryLou. The year-long process of helping to shape these ideas was a crucible of how she has strengthened me as a person and leader during our forty-nine years together. From youth pastor to university president, it has always been a team effort. Without her astuteness and insights, coupled with encompassing love, I would have failed as a leader early on.

Finally, my kids contributed more to this book than they will ever know. Grady and Madison, along with their mom, keep me grounded in what matters most. Being "Dad" is a job I love, although it is lots tougher than being a university president. Now that my kids are twenty-somethings, our lives sometimes cross like ships in the night, but their love, care, laughter, quirkiness, and grace only get more delightful with every passing year.

Above all, thanks be to God for giving me the opportunity to serve through leadership. The Lord has honored me with an astonishing fulfillment of the benediction promise we recite at each campus chapel service, *"No eye has seen, no ear has heard, no mind has conceived what God has prepared for those who love Him."*

The author's royalties from the sale of this book
are donated to the non-profit *Foundation for Christian Learning*
for the support of Christian education and scholarships.

Part 1

OPPORTUNITY LEADERSHIP CHANGES EVERYTHING

For my thoughts are not your thoughts,
    neither are your ways my ways, declares the LORD.
For as the heavens are higher than the earth,
    so are my ways higher than your ways
    and my thoughts than your thoughts.
(Isa. 55:8–9 ESV)

Chapter 1

A New Model for Ministry Leadership

A s a Christian university president, I never *planned* to:

- start an NCAA football program from scratch
- launch a school of nursing as a result of our "old main" building falling down
- develop the world's premier Christian University for the Arts
- build a network of branch campuses across the South, and then close most of them years later
- create the largest online Christian university MBA program in China
- develop a campus community that is a beacon for racial reconciliation in the Deep South

The most critical turning points and breakthroughs of ministry are rarely planned. I can prove that to you if you hang in there with me for the first few pages of this book.

In 2002, I purposely began to let go of the iron grip all leaders have on planning as the foundation of focus and energy. It was a struggle that took over a decade until, as a university, we were entirely driven by *capturing opportunities* rather than *building plans.*

Paradoxically, relinquishing planning is the single best thing I've ever done in my professional ministry life—and also the scariest. It was complex to accomplish but also simple. And, even though it took a long time to implement, it changed everything overnight.

My evolution away from dependency on traditional planning was worth it all. This shift opened up growth, reach, and ministry that would never have been imaginable if I had stayed welded to conventional planning. And, as a bonus, it has brought a personal joy and freedom in leadership that I never thought possible.

> RELINQUISHING PLANNING IS THE SINGLE BEST THING I'VE EVER DONE IN MY PROFESSIONAL MINISTRY LIFE—AND ALSO THE SCARIEST.

Opportunity Leadership—the model of leadership that I've developed as I've shifted focus away from traditional planning—is almost bewildering to those who have never experienced it. I'm often asked questions like:

- How is it possible to provide leadership without a plan for the future?

- How do you gain buy-in from stakeholders without a planning structure?

- How do you get agreement on where you are headed, measure your effectiveness, or even know what's next without a plan?

I've learned that the only way to convince skeptics of Opportunity Leadership is to show them the results.

COVID-19 is the most straightforward example of why traditional planning is ineffective. Did your ministry plan for it? Did anyone? Of course not! But we all dealt with it, made adjustments rapidly, and even found ways to significantly improve our "normal ministry"—even though a simultaneous worldwide pandemic was not included in the five-year plan of a single ministry leader.

When the virus hit, every long-range organizational plan was tossed in the trash, and we all became stronger leaders because we couldn't depend on a pre-determined plan to cope with this challenge. Instead, this "opportunity of crisis" required us to provide leadership through it. And most importantly, we all became more dependent on God for the future rather than leaning on our carefully crafted plans.

For ministries, the jarring and speedy adjustments we made during COVID-19 were a forced push to step into the core of Opportunity Leadership. It's a model of leadership that begins and ends with complete trust in God for a ministry's direction. It allows future destinations to be ordered by His hand and loosens our iron grip on the wheel of control. When we embrace it, we join those leaders who have become free from the overwhelming burden of determining what is best for their ministry. We no longer need to manipulate our efforts and circumstances to engineer outcomes that force pre-determined destinations to be reached.

Opportunity Leadership is grounded in waiting in anticipation for God-given opportunities to develop that mesh seamlessly with our mission, gifting, and capacity—propelling us to destinations that are heavenly ordained. As a result, we become leaders who hone traits that enable us to become highly sensitive to the wind of God and create an organizational culture that allows us to respond to new opportunities with urgency, adeptness, and energy.

Proof That Opportunity Leadership Works

If you've been schooled in the practices of leadership, I know you're already skeptical that leading without a plan is possible. Let me start by addressing any initial doubts you have about my challenge to discard planning. After that, I'll demonstrate why Opportunity Leadership is a superior path.

Following the organizational patterns developed by the corporate community, most ministry leaders are so deeply embedded in traditional planning structures that these ideas may appear on the page like a foreign language. But I assure you, even leaders in the most bureaucratic structures can implement at least small portions of this model—and the slightest movement toward Opportunity Leadership will be uplifting for you and your ministry.

> OPPORTUNITY LEADERSHIP IS GROUNDED IN WAITING FOR GOD-GIVEN OPPORTUNITIES TO DEVELOP THAT MESH SEAMLESSLY WITH YOUR MISSION, GIFTING, AND CALLING.

I'd never before seen leadership unbuckled from planning and had to find my way in the dark. You won't have to because you'll get the benefit of learning from my experience. I'll outline the why, who, and how of implementing the model based on my years of developing Opportunity Leadership by trial and error. You'll be encouraged that making the shifts necessary to embrace the entirety of the Opportunity Leadership model requires a slow, gradual, and purposeful change and is not best accomplished with dramatic acceleration or sharp turns. And to help you chart your path, I'll share the war stories—good and bad—for how Opportunity Leadership gets lived out because this is an in-the-trenches practical model for leaders like you.

One caution, though. Don't worry about getting a clear answer to the end-point question of how you're going to do this in your current leadership role—that's planning. Instead, just start by capturing the opportunities for change that are easily grasped in the low-hanging fruit of the model, and then let the rest work itself out with time—that's Opportunity Leadership.

Now, let's look at the proof that this leadership model really works.

In our early years of living by the Opportunity Leadership

principles as a university, I was stopped cold after writing a grant request to a foundation. The application asked for a summary of the significant accomplishments of the previous five years. Not thinking much about it, I quickly jotted down those advances that stood out in my memory. But when I saw all that God had done written down on a single piece of paper, I was overwhelmed.

I knew right then that I had to devise a creative way to share with my board of trustees the same astonishment and celebrate God's blessings. Here's how it happened.

As a university, we don't do planning—we capture opportunities. For years the board had been 100 percent supportive of Opportunity Leadership, so looks of confusion shrouded the room when I laid before them what appeared to be a five-year aggressive comprehensive plan for the university.

In the style of a traditional planning leadership model, the document focused on five significant overarching goals, along with a list of seventy-two implementation targets. At most universities, a board would look at the paper with excitement to see what might be ahead and prepare to work with the president to launch an eighteen-month-long series of discussions across the campus to refine the goals and objectives list and gain input and buy-in from all sectors of stakeholders.

But my board studied the document before them with puzzlement. They knew I didn't believe in what I identify as "destination planning" and that, as a university, we had purposefully made the shift completely away from the long-range planning model that has become a fortress for nearly all leaders. As a board, we had talked repeatedly over the previous years about our commitment to stop projecting God's destinations, but instead build a faith, philosophy, and team

> OPPORTUNITY LEADERSHIP IS THE ART OF ACHIEVING YOUR MISSION BY CAPTURING CHANGE INSTEAD OF CREATING IT.

that is sensitive to the wind of God and moves quickly to capture opportunities when it blows. Our remarkable success in the preceding years was a result of Opportunity Leadership. It was the hallmark on which we had built our future as a university.

Despite their questioning looks, I pressed on with my presentation, beginning to read aloud the goals of the five-year plan, even though I could almost hear the board members' silent reactions of alarm in response to the bold benchmarks.

Belhaven University Five-Year Goals

1. Increase enrollment 43 percent

   Impossible! This would make us one of the fastest-growing universities in the country.

2. Raise $21 million

   Crazy!!! This is way too much money for us to raise that fast. Let's do a feasibility study.

3. Construct $32 million of new buildings and renovations

   Now, this is getting out of hand. Our job as a board is to slow this president WAY down.

4. Add seven undergraduate academic majors, including nursing, computer science, film, and social work

   Nursing in itself is huge. How about two or maybe three majors, and then see how we are doing?

5. Add eight graduate degrees, including dance, education, and leadership

   Let's skinny this up, so we don't frustrate the faculty with failure because we took on too much.

As I read the first couple of goals, the look of disorientation turned to distress and anxiety. As I got through the third goal, I began to see smiles on the faces of some of the longest-serving board members who figured out where I was going. And, by the time I'd finished announcing the fifth goal, all except the newest members realized what was happening.

The presentation was not a *projection* of the next five years. Instead, what I gave the board was a summary of what had been accomplished during the *previous* five years—a time during which we operated without a plan and focused on capturing opportunities.

Opportunity Leadership had changed everything for our university. If we had stayed cemented to traditional planning, and I had brought the same goals to our board five years previously (before they actually happened), their reaction would have been predictable:

1. The board would have questioned my ability as a leader because the plan was far too ambitious. Bluntly, they would have thought I was foolish or naive to recommend goals this bold.

2. The board would have cut the five-year goals in about half—and at best, our results would have been about half of what we actually achieved over those five years.

Plus, we would never have been amazed by what only God could do because we would have limited the plan to what we knew we could accomplish. And, we certainly wouldn't have gone on to add "with God's help" into the university's brochure.

This hard-results demonstration cemented our commitment to abandoning traditional planning and moving ahead with a confidence that God will bring us opportunities—although we have no idea what they might be. And since the time of this five-year validation, I've learned that surprises at this level were only the beginning of opportunities that the Lord would bring our way when we fully committed to Opportunity Leadership.

So gather your courage, set aside assumed leadership absolutes, cut up the box, and let's walk together to start capturing change rather than creating it. This book is the story of Opportunity Leadership lived out and it will help you do just that. It is not an idealized theoretical model of leadership, but a proven fresh approach to leadership that will free you from the confinement of traditional planning and bring you the joy of leading by catching the wind of God and trusting Him for both the opportunities and outcomes.

It is time for more Christian leaders to stop planning and start getting results!

Chapter 2

Are You Simply Going Through the Motions?

On a Monday morning, I called the assistant of another university president. I wanted to set up a few minutes to talk about a potential partnership that would allow us both to reach a significant pool of new students and provide a substantial new source of income. After some explanation to assure I was not selling something and was a colleague in the presidency, I was told that there might be a gap in the president's schedule to chat in about two weeks.

Emphasizing that this opportunity had urgency, I asked if I could speak with the president for only twenty minutes sometime in the next two days. I simply wanted to get the discussion started. "His schedule is packed with meetings because we are working on a master plan," was the reply. But I was told he might be able to squeeze in a brief time late on Friday afternoon.

I hung up and called a different university whose president took my call without an appointment. This president was responsive to the opportunity of partnership and overjoyed to reach the additional students, plus make good use of the new revenue projected to be over $1 million annually.

My experience with the first president's assistant helps illustrate how the traditional planning process is totally consuming, and too often becomes an end in itself. It keeps leaders extremely busy and brings few meaningful results. Leading a ministry through the well-worn path of planning has:

- key team members packing too many tedious meetings into every day

- administrators collecting far too much tangential data

- CEOs attempting to cajole buy-in from the most fearful people controlling the edges of a stake-holding community with an iron grip because of a lack of trust

And, if success is measured by "getting it past the committee" instead of the inspiration of a new direction, there is something wrong with both the ethos and edifice of a planning model.

MANY LEADERS ARE PRIVATELY FRUSTRATED WITH THE INEFFICIENCY OF GRINDING AWAY IN A PLANNING PROCESS. STILL, THEY CLING TO IT WITH TENACITY BECAUSE NO OTHER ALTERNATIVE GUARANTEES RECOGNITION OF THEIR "VALUE-ADDED" AS THE LEADER.

Although appearing diligent, and I'm sure well-intentioned, many leaders are only going through the motions of leadership because the results are typically inadequate. They are reduced to the lowest common denominators of agreement, security, and manageability, and overlaid with an idealized vision of the future. These leaders are privately frustrated with the inefficiency of grinding away in a planning process. Still, they cling to it with tenacity because no other alternative (other than extraordinary fundraising) guarantees recognition of their "value-added" as the leader. So, they retain a broken model for fear that they would appear to be abandoning their leadership role if they eliminated it.

As a result, they fill their days with a schedule that doesn't produce deliverable results but still feel justified in their role by the constant activity that keeps them harried. And too often, they are pushing forward the weighty structure of planning, even when they know, deep down, that it probably won't make much of a difference.

Why We Allow Empty Planning to Fill Our Time

Maybe you can relate to the leaders I just described. You are diligent and want to make a difference in your ministry, but sometimes you feel like you're going through the motions. So why do leaders continue to follow the traditional model of planning? There are many intertwined reasons why we so dutifully follow it—and, as a result, segregate our dependence on God to a prayer at the beginning of the planning meeting, a blessing over our plan when the work is completed, and an impassioned lament when the plan doesn't work. I would suggest ten factors that are pushing us to cling to superfluous formal planning structures.

1. We Embrace Planning to Please Board Members

At its most practical level, ministry leaders embrace complex planning to resonate with board members' everyday corporate culture. Structured strategic planning fits the board's expectations of what a leader should do because it mirrors their world's best practices. The board members are the ones who "own" the ministry—but because they cannot be involved in the depth of a leader's work, formalized planning provides a tangible way for them to stamp control on the organization.

2. We Assume Planning Equals Leadership

As Christian leaders, we have been indoctrinated with the assumption that planning equals leadership. Of course, we have a responsibility to be out in front of wherever the ministry is going. But I would argue that our vital role is in facilitating excellence in the execution of the direction we already know we're headed, rather than trying to predict destinations of the future.

If we were all judged on our ability to plan a future, most of us would be considered miserable failures if we were to judge by how far off-mark our idealized plan misses the target. So why would we want to continue to make future planning our centerpiece?

3. We Are Expected to Distinctly Hear from God

As spiritual leaders, there is an assumption that God will uniquely speak to us in ways that make clear the ministry's direction. Because of that, many ministries are waiting in whispered expectation for their leader to demonstrate unique spiritual insight at a level that empowers them to see around corners predicting the future with pinpoint accuracy. And in some theological traditions, this characteristic is openly measured in valuing ministry leadership.

Of course, spiritual discernment needs to be in a leader's gifting, and spiritual leadership must be an evident hallmark of our work. Although most often, we need to demonstrate our spiritual acumen through our relationships rather than by unveiling plans.

4. We Believe Leaders Are the Keepers of Order, Structure, Equity, and Process

We often feel our leadership is hitting on all cylinders when plans (and people) fit into orderly building blocks of progress that can be arranged in equal parts. But moving a ministry forward involves considering intertwined complex issues that often won't neatly align. There are personnel strengths and weaknesses, resource priorities and projections, bias or blind spots, competing priorities, and more. Those are not decisions best made in a diverse group setting when the agenda is most often controlled by whoever speaks first or most forcefully.

Helpful solutions are rarely found in orderly planning that ignites territorialism by bringing each attendee to the table advocating for their unique constituency group. Such settings are doomed to mediocrity because meaningful change may only be discussed in carefully nuanced tones for fear of misinterpretation.

5. We Have Bought Into the False Dichotomy of Leadership Versus Administration

I don't know how many times I've heard the misguided declaration, "I'm a leader, not an administrator." Does this mean there is something nobler about leadership than administration? Does this mean only the smartest can lead while the others can only administrate? When boiled down, the most effective ministry CEOs probably spend, at most, about 10 percent of their time engaged in moments of "pure leadership," and all the rest of their work is administration. One is not better than the other—both are vitally important in leadership.

> LEADERSHIP IS NOT ABOUT PUNCHING THE "LEADERSHIP CLOCK" VERSUS THE "ADMINISTRATION CLOCK." IT IS ABOUT BEING READY WHEN THE CLOCK STRIKES.

Leadership without administrative execution is hollow. In the critical tipping point moments of leadership decisions (about a dozen decisions will make or break the year for most CEOs), you will not have the wisdom to lead unless you've already gained the insight only available by in-the-weeds administration. Leadership is not about punching the "leadership clock" versus the "administration clock." It is about being ready when the clock strikes.

6. We Assume Buy-In Requires Including All Stakeholders in the Planning Process

We wrongly suppose the only way to get ministry-wide buy-in is to include all key stakeholders in a planning process. But if having a seat at the planning table is the only way to get a voice in an organization, significant inward examination needs to precede any outward look through a planning lens. A culture of transparency of information, accessibility to those in authority, and a purposeful nonhierarchical culture all create an atmosphere where ideas can be shared and explored, ownership created, and insights gained from everyone across the spectrum of the ministry.

7. We Have Been Programmed to Accept That "Planning Takes Time"

"Planning takes time" is another defective leaning-post of leaders. Some of the most direction-setting decisions I've been involved with have happened within weeks of the original idea being proposed. I've also walked through substantial changes from consideration to implementation within just hours because opportunity afforded a window of response that would have been missed by delaying.

When the right organizational environment is created, planning structures and meetings no longer need to be the dominant activity of leaders. Instead, enriching the culture and empowering people becomes a leader's priority.

8. We Conclude That Planning Is the Only Way to Visibly Lead

Vacuums do become filled, so some leaders live under the erroneous assumption that they will lose their platform to lead if they are not visibly controlling. Opportunity Leadership is not suggesting that planning be abolished altogether. Instead, it seeks a different source for the plans.

Rather than committees, conference tables, and whiteboards,

planning revolves around a constant interaction with both the significant issues and the minutia, out of which new insights, solutions, and opportunities will be revealed and captured. These may come from us as the CEOs, but probably not.

As leaders, we're responsible for helping to sort out good ideas from bad ones, prioritizing time and energy, and using our muscle of position to push past the objections, fears, silos, and possessiveness. And then, we set a high standard for implementation.

9. We Assume Measuring Results Should Drive Our Planning

There is a school of leadership demanding that everything we do organizationally must be measured, and thus, planning is built around our ability to audit outcomes. There are two problems with this approach. First, we rarely do it. We promise our donors the moon, but never return and report why most of our moon-shots didn't even come close. Second, we are only playing around the edges of the most meaningful aspects of ministry when measurement becomes our guiding priority.

It is time to put away props of leadership and not be wooed by the immediacy of appearing productive by PowerPoints jammed with endless data or multi-year projection graphs. Instead, our standard for how we measure success as Christian leadership needs to reflect the desires of God, built on spiritual values that endure. Or to say it even more bluntly, consider the rebuke of God to His people in Amos 5:21–24 as expressed in The Message translation:

I can't stand your religious meetings.
    I'm fed up with your conferences and conventions.
I want nothing to do with your religion projects,
    your pretentious slogans and goals.
I'm sick of your fund-raising schemes,
    your public relations and image making.

I've had all I can take of your noisy ego-music.
When was the last time you sang to *me?*
Do you know what I want?
I want justice—oceans of it.
I want fairness—rivers of it.
That's what I want. That's *all* I want.

When I look back on my years of leading Belhaven University, I count success by watching students whose lives were dramatically transformed as they captured God's best for their future, and faculty who have deeply invested in developing insightful worldview thinking and Christ-like mentoring and grace. I also see chapel services during which the Lord spoke to us all in deepening ways, athletic teams and residence halls living that purposely built character, and God-centered racial reconciliation lived out every day in every interaction. Those successes don't show in graphs or charts, but they are how God looks at the value of our university.

IT IS TIME TO PUT AWAY PROPS OF LEADERSHIP AND NOT BE WOOED BY THE IMMEDIACY OF APPEARING PRODUCTIVE BY POWERPOINTS JAMMED WITH ENDLESS DATA OR MULTI-YEAR PROJECTION GRAPHS.

10. We Believe Failure Comes from Failing to Plan

We accept the long-quoted consultant's refrain, "Those who fail to plan, plan to fail." I completely disagree. The more reliant we are on planning for our guidance, the less dependent we are on the fountainhead of wisdom. Stepping back from the busyness of planning requires an enormous dependence on God—not just prayer for the blessing of our decisions or rescue from the current crisis. We must become utterly dependent on the Lord for our entire future, both personally and professionally.

That is a scary step for many Christian leaders, so we cling to the few Scriptures demonstrating detailed planning, such as Jesus instructing His disciples to prepare the Last Supper or Nehemiah rebuilding the walls of Jerusalem. Yet, at the same time, we are quick to overlook how often God gave the *biggest* ideas to His people in dreams—from Joseph, Jacob, and Abraham, to the wise men seeking Christ, or John on the Isle of Patmos. As Christian leaders, we need to spend more time listening, dreaming, and praying to find God's destinations for our ministry future, rather than laboring at whiteboards attempting to draw out schematics of God's best for us.

Breaking Free from the Magnetic Pull of Planning

Your calling and responsibility are too important for your days to be swallowed up in going through the motions of leadership. Unless we purposefully detach, the irresistible magnetic force of planning will control our productivity, priorities, and prestige.

Take a hard and honest look back at your calendar. Last year, how much time did you invest in planning that genuinely moved the needle? Seriously—count up the days, trips, meetings, reading, writing, and worry.

Unfortunately, the blunt answer won't be encouraging because I've seen this consumption-by-planning pattern in hundreds of ministries, with most producing lots of lofty promises but underwhelming results. We must get past our dependency on traditional planning structures to break free to find the future God has in store for us.

The day that we, as leaders, stop worrying about justifying our positions, expertise, value-added, or salary because of our role in destination planning is when God will bring opportunities that open doors to a future we never dreamed possible.

Chapter 3

The Big Idea–
Sailboats Versus
Powerboats

The capacity to take a complex idea and communicate it simply is one of the most essential gifts of effective leaders. That bold vision of a big idea then takes root when coupled with the commitment to share the same explanation repeatedly to each new listener with the same level of passion, whether it's the first time or the thousandth time to tell the story. If big ideas can't easily be passed along to be assimilated and implemented, they will never take root and will wither.

The big idea of Opportunity Leadership is exceptionally complex to comprehend without experience living out this leadership model. Only confusion will rule the day if you expect your stakeholders to be enthusiastic when you suggest to them, "Let's bring an end to the mountains of effort we've put into strategic planning for years and years, disband all the committees, and stop working toward five- or ten-year goals. Instead, we're going to be still and wait for God to bring us opportunities." That won't fly—unless you can explain it simply so others can "see" the vision.

I use a metaphor of a powerboat versus a sailboat to draw an image illuminating the dramatic difference between traditional strategic planning and Opportunity Leadership. My concise message to explain the contrast is this word-picture I've shared thousands and thousands of times through the years:

> In ministry leadership, we have a fundamental choice to make—and although the answer is easy, the implementation is difficult:

1. Would we rather try to achieve a set of ambitious goals by revving up the engines of our ministry powerboats to create the best programs, structures, benchmarks, and future our well-informed collective thinking can imagine?

or

2. Would we rather find our destination in sailboats, prepared and equipped to catch the wind of God and to go only wherever that wind might take us?

While the second choice is clearly our desire, too often we plan, work, and lead as if our ministry direction is totally dependent on the power we can generate and the best course we can envision.

We may feel proud when powerboats of ministry are big, well built, and polished, but even a small, poorly crafted, and worn sailboat will outdistance a powerboat every time—because only the sailboat can catch the wind of God.

That is the message. All the rest is details.

> WE MAY FEEL PROUD WHEN POWERBOATS OF MINISTRY ARE BIG, WELL BUILT, AND POLISHED, BUT EVEN A SMALL, POORLY CRAFTED, AND WORN SAILBOAT WILL OUTDISTANCE A POWERBOAT EVERY TIME—BECAUSE ONLY THE SAILBOAT CAN CATCH THE WIND OF GOD.

If you come to my campus and stop any employee on the sidewalk and ask about planning, they would all be able to explain to you the core concept of Opportunity Leadership (although they probably won't use that label) by describing the picture of powerboats versus sailboats. They also might draw out that image by highlighting that sailboats are exciting and far-reaching, but powerboats are not only limited in range but also dependability. They might further talk about the hard work needed to be prepared to catch the wind of God when the breeze begins to blow versus the expediency of a gas-and-go powerboat whose structure can easily ignore the wind to go where we plan to go.

From the campus operations team to the board of trustees, we all have embraced the big idea of Opportunity Leadership. But it wasn't always that way.

Trading in a Powerboat for a Sailboat

Like craving a heaping plate of the best Southern comfort food, including bread pudding for dessert, most ministry leaders and boards find their consolation in developing complex planning systems. As a leader, I was right in the middle of that pack for years, clinging to a traditional planning model as a demonstration of my leadership. From my well-worn path of graduate work in higher education administration, to college and university governance, to adapting the best thinking of business, I joined that army of lock-step leaders who believed we could not possibly go forward as a ministry without a concise, clearly articulated five- or ten-year plan that projected a bold future to direct our path, inspire our stakeholders, and motivate our givers.

Traditionally, from the announcement of the planning team launch to the production of a finished document, the model demands about a year-and-a-half of intense, multi-layered, complex effort. This process is nearly always guided by a "Blue Ribbon Committee" with the appropriate subcommittees, so no stakeholder group is left out. It is filled with enough compromise to ensure everybody gets at least a small bite of the apple.

At the end of it all, the plan is always written around a theme that allows each point to be summarized with a word beginning with the same letter. The goals are graphically presented in smoothly sloping growth-inspiring projections that only foresee dramatic success. The final document contains new initiatives that look symmetrical in the brochure and make absolutely everyone connected somewhat satisfied that their priority is included.

The five to ten objectives then project a future bold enough to inspire donors and give the board assurance they oversee something sophisticated. Plus, to top it off, the CEO promises to measure the results (which we never actually report). And finally, by the time the planned future doesn't materialize as projected, it is time to appoint another Blue Ribbon planning committee to begin the cycle again.

> WE NEED THE COURAGE TO BREAK THIS CYCLE OF DEPENDENCY ON THE POWERBOAT OF PLANNING AND INSTEAD PUT OUR TRUST IN THE SAILBOATS OF OPPORTUNITY PREPARED TO GO WHEREVER THE WIND OF GOD MIGHT TAKE US.

We, as leaders, need the courage to break this cycle of dependency on the powerboat of planning and instead put our trust in the sailboats of opportunity that are prepared to go wherever the wind of God might take us. Traditional planning, at best, severely limits our potential, and at worst, drains energy from ministries.

The implementation of the brightest plans we can envision is only a small glimmer of where God would lead us if we loosen our grip on attempting to control the future.

Before going further, it is essential to highlight a critical distinction in planning. The powerboating effort that consumes far too much time, energy, and focus is *destination planning*. I am advocating the abandonment of predicting futures through planning structures. Instead, I'm encouraging a deeper investment in *implementation planning*. This completely different focus puts our energy into getting the most from our current portfolio of responsibility and subsequently relying only on the wind of God to propel our sailboats to new destinations.

The Differences Between Sailboats and Powerboats

I once wanted to buy a McGregor boat, which is the only saltwater craft on the market that also functions like a powerboat. I really wanted to sail, but didn't always want to be limited by how the wind was blowing. Plus, I also wanted to fish in shallow water. I studied the pictures and configurations of their boat for hours. I called the dealer and even traveled several states away to inspect one model in person. And then I talked to real sailors—and had my dreams crushed.

If a boat preserves the structure of a powerboat to retain its predictability, the vessel becomes an extremely unresponsive sailboat. And to make matters worse, if you want to sail freely in response to the wind, the boat won't get near the fish because of limited shallow-water maneuvering capacity. In other words, I found that I had to make a decision: either buy a sailboat or a powerboat. I couldn't straddle the line.

Many ministries are attempting to operate with a foot in each boat. We desire to completely trust in God, while at the same time limiting our future to the outcomes of our structured planning models. Pick one! Just like boats, attempting to capture the strengths of both models will minimize the value of the whole.

If you'll picture the sailboat versus powerboat metaphor more specifically, it provides a stark contrast of Opportunity Leadership versus traditional strategic planning. I've detailed these six characteristics more extensively in my book *The Longview: Lasting Strategies for Rising Leaders*[1] but include this summary as a starting point for understanding these distinctions. Each key benchmark reinforces the decision to choose one craft over the other and highlights the dramatic difference in how we approach the future.

1. Trust

> *Choosing a sailboat or a powerboat begins with*
> *the core decision of where we place our trust.*

In sailing, we trust the wind to propel and guide us, and we must gear everything we do around being responsive to the wind's direction, strength, and consistency. In contrast, in a powerboat, we trust in the motor to give us power, bearing, and stamina. In it, we can easily ignore or even go against the wind because our course is self-determined by our horsepower.

We will be consumed by confusion until we settle once-and-for-all that our trust is only in Christ, and our ministry functions and operations are built around that core understanding.

2. Focus

> *Sailing calls for attentiveness to everything going on around*
> *us, while a powerboat permits us to be internally focused.*

On a sailboat, we don't simply respond to the direction of the wind. We must listen to the wind and watch how the boat interacts with the wind. And further, each part of a sailboat has a pivotal function to ensure the whole operates effectively. The awareness needed to sail demands focus that is always looking up and looking out.

In a powerboat, we hear only the motor. The wind is ignored because the motor's power and its fine-tuned engine are propelling us to new destinations. While at full speed, our focus is not up and out, but inward, as the power of the motor overwhelms us, and finding optimal speed and stability becomes our focus.

3. Preparation

Sailing requires constant preparation, while a powerboat is an immediate-response cruiser.

Sailing is complex and takes training, experience, and lots of practice to become equipped to handle all weather conditions. Further, a sailboat requires ongoing careful maintenance to ensure it is ready when needed. The highest level sailors spend more time preparing than they do on the water, and in that meticulous preparation, they are ready to reach top speeds at sea.

In contrast, the immediate gratification of a powerboat usually only needs a tank of gas to be ready to jump to top speeds. There are few interconnected parts, and as long as the motor is strong, it can keep moving despite other deficiencies.

4. Control

A large sailboat demands teamwork with a mix of intertwined skills, while a powerboat allows isolation.

Yacht racing is one of the most fascinating sports. Crews are highly schooled and practiced to move and adjust in harmony as they maintain top speeds. The interconnectedness of the boat's key elements, along with the operational team, work in synchronization as the boat adjusts to weather conditions, abrupt turns, and wind speeds.

At the other end of the spectrum, a powerboat operator is entirely self-sufficient. Even in larger boats, one person can set the course, change the direction, or adjust the speed. It not only enables, but encourages, isolation to operate efficiently.

5. Direction

*The bearing and speed of the wind determine the course
of a sailboat, while a hand on the wheel turns a powerboat
in any direction.*

A sailboat has limitless endurance, as long as it doesn't fight the wind. Being responsive to what the wind "gives it," a sailboat can track a lengthy course, although it must always be ready to shift and adjust as the wind changes. The captain may feel empowered with a hand on the wheel guiding the vessel, but that control is only granted in response to the wind. Pushing too far against the wind will nearly always trigger disastrous results.

Likewise, the speed of a powerboat is impressive—until it runs out of gas. It can produce enormous spurts of power, but they are limited in their endurance. And although a powerboat can be abruptly maneuvered in all environments, there is always a finite limit to its energy source.

6. Relationships

*A sailboat's beauty and splendor are admired in all waters,
while a powerboat is often unwelcome.*

A sailboat a hundred yards offshore will stop every beachcomber to watch, as they imagine the peace and tranquility of being onboard. It attracts people's attention, interest, and imagination as it glides through the water with strength and beauty. A sailboat is always a welcome sight because it does not leave pollution or wake that troubles other boaters or wildlife.

The contamination, noise, and disruption of a powerboat don't bother those in front of its path, but can anger those behind. The wake of a speedboat upsets all that have to combat its disturbance of the water. Its noise can be overwhelming for those nearby, and it is continually leaving pollution trailing in the waters wherever it travels.

7. Demands

Sailing does not provide a lazy thoughtless day on the water, but demands all-out effort, while a powerboat offers a comfortable way to act like a sailor without putting in the work.

Sailing is challenging, demanding, and unpredictable, and should only be attempted by those committed to becoming genuine sailors. Effectiveness in all conditions requires a high level of learning, insight, experience, anticipation, and attention to detail. Preparation is foundational to success, and understanding both the wind and the boat and how they interact is critical in reaching new destinations.

Almost anyone can jump in a powerboat and call themselves a sailor. Very little instruction, experience, planning, or focus is necessary to get moving on the water. Destinations can be reached without extensive effort or deliberation, as long as the motor is running strong and the tank is full of gas.

Don't Just Rock the Boat—Get a New One

Finally, to close the loop on the story about my boat choice, I eventually bought a small nineteen-foot powerboat to fish the Gulf Coast's intercoastal waterway. After months of research, I determined I just didn't have the patience for sailing, and I didn't want to put in the work required to have a sailboat ready for the few days I could use it.

The demands of sailing must be understood in the hard reality of choosing a sailboat over a powerboat. Likewise, moving from traditional strategic

WHEN WE CAPTURE OPPORTUNITIES RATHER THAN PREDICT DESTINATIONS, WE ARE AT THE HELM OF A VESSEL THAT CAUSES EVERYONE IN OUR SPHERE OF INFLUENCE TO STOP, LOOK UP, AND BE LONGINGLY DRAWN TO OUR MINISTRY.

planning to Opportunity Leadership and trusting God entirely for direction doesn't make our task easier. I think it is tougher, especially in the early stages of learning to sail, to hold to that commitment and not yield to the tempting default of familiar patterns of organizational practice.

I'm convinced Opportunity Leadership is a biblical model for leadership because I have seen it work with remarkable results. I know that in *capturing opportunities* rather than *predicting destinations*, we are at the helm of a vessel that causes everyone in our sphere of influence to stop, look up, and be longingly drawn to our ministry.

Chapter 4

Sea Legs or Seasickness

Where do you expect the university to be in five or ten years?" is a question I am asked regularly. That's a very natural question to ask of any CEO because society expects leaders to have a "vision" for the future. And, we've been schooled to believe that we must lavishly articulate that vision in measurable outcomes.

When asked that question, my response is—and this is the absolute blunt answer which I've even shared in television news interviews—"I have no idea. But I do know that the best plan we could come up with around conference tables pales in comparison to the plan that God has in store for us."

Candidly, I don't know what our future as a university looks like. We may have more students five or ten years from now, or fewer students. I don't know what new academic programs we might add or cut. I don't know where we might open new campuses or close some. I don't plan the future. Our destination is totally dependent on God bringing us opportunities. And so, not only don't I plan for the future, but even more importantly, *I don't worry about it.*

Based on history and the shaping of cultural and market forces, I could easily speculate about what the future might hold, but I don't plan for a specific future, nor do I work to hit specific growth targets. Having lived Opportunity Leadership for many years now, I know that when I look back to consider what I might have anticipated five or ten years ago, today's reality will look nothing like the future I could have imagined at the time.

Instead of destination planning, what we must plan well is the execution of our implementation agenda. At my university, we teach English, hold chapel services, play soccer, provide food service, pay the bills, and complete all the other functions that go into running a small city on a campus. We plan and work hard to ensure those activities are robust, efficient, seamless, and effective. It is good stewardship to plan well what we know we are responsible for doing, and I believe God won't entrust us with more if we don't use well what we already hold in our portfolio.

> THE BEST PLAN WE COULD COME UP WITH AROUND CONFERENCE TABLES PALES IN COMPARISON TO THE PLAN THAT GOD HAS IN STORE FOR US.

This type of implementation planning must be developed as "locally" as possible, with the people in the trenches carrying out the specific work. In contrast, comprehensive visionary plans are often drawn up by boards, CEOs, and strategic task forces. Then those leaders spend the following months or years in frustration because the frontline implementers can't move the changes forward with the same seamlessness envisioned by the planning team.

Rather than a formalized planning model drawing out the future in the machine-precision schematics of a powerboat, we need to be leading with the fluid nature of a sailboat, in which the whole is dependent on the effectiveness of each unique part. The mainsail, headsail, spinnaker, rudder, and tiller, along with each halyard, gunwale, cleat, beam, jib, batten, and the dozens of other parts of a sailing vessel, are deeply dependent on each other. When properly interconnected, we create a ship of strength and endurance prepared to catch the wind of God.

As leaders, we find our true calling when we break free from a traditional planning process anchored in structure, stability, and control. Instead, we focus on being attentive, informed, and flexible enough to ensure that each vital part of the sailboat works together as smoothly as possible. Skilled leaders know when and how to helpfully intervene when the ropes become tangled and sails twisted, or critical parts become corroded and worn and need to be refurbished or replaced.

Unintended Outcomes of Destination Planning

The church has learned to build powerboats that often mirror the impressiveness of those constructed by the business world. But unlike secular institutions, our eternal focus values the quality of the journey, not simply establishing new beachheads. Structured destination planning not only limits what we might accomplish, but the nature of the process creates five by-products that pollute a ministry's organizational culture.

1. Destination Planning Rarely Produces the Most Significant Outcomes in Our Ministry

Look back on the last decade of your ministry. What was the most significant outcome? Was it drawn out in a plan? Maybe a new building was planned, or one new initiative. But did you prepare for that key new employee who has made all the difference? Did you plan for the successes you most talk about with donors today? Did a new vital ministry area emerge because you planned it from scratch months or years in advance, or did unexpected opportunities open those doors?

Unless you are way outside the norm, what is significant is rarely envisioned through a formal planning structure. And if you answer that the planning structure did work and produced exactly what you expected, then I'd make the case you probably missed the best things

God had for you because your powerboat was ignoring the wind of God when it blew in your direction.

2. Destination Planning Homogenizes Your Strengths and Enables Mediocrity

In a planning process, everyone must be included, but if you're treating every gift of your ministry of equal value, you're missing your God-given calling and gifts. At my university, God opened the opportunity for us to become a leader in the arts (that story is coming later). In those early days of building our university, we woefully lacked in many key areas. Still, we were beginning to develop an exceptional dance program at a time when no other Christ-centered university offered a dance major. Capitalizing on that strength, we promoted it, funded it, staffed it, and built top-quality facilities for it. And this was all at the same time our football team was playing on a borrowed high school field and our STEM program was working with antiquated equipment.

If we had entrusted our future to the traditional strategic planning process, no stakeholder group would ever have promoted such lavish expenses for dance when we were woefully understaffed and under-funded in other important academic departments. But God wasn't bringing us the opportunities in these other areas as He did in dance. His wind was blowing to create something dramatic for Christians in dance, and our little sailboat captured the moment. And since that time, our dance program has brought national and international visibility to our campus. Focusing on the opportunity to build on this strength has "lifted all the boats" as we've been able to grow the whole of the institution on the reputation of our dance department.

3. Destination Planning Primarily Focuses on Deficiencies

Yes, your planning structure will probably include a SWOT analysis that attempts to align your strengths. But planning by nature primarily focuses on what you don't have rather than celebrating what you've been given. Opportunity Leadership flips the table, setting your attention on the change that comes from God's blowing wind, while also learning to be satisfied that other needs are being met for now as God intends. Planning that accentuates your shortcomings, rather than rejoicing in your blessings, is not creating a culture for expanded reach and growth—or building the ministry-wide thankful spirit that honors God. To replace deficiency-focused planning with opportunity-focused anticipation, the testimony of Paul in Philippians 4 must become engrained in our outlook and actions on two levels.

First, we must avoid the trap that allows planning to become a structure for collective worry. "Don't worry about anything; instead, pray about everything. Tell God what you need, and thank him for all he has done. Then you will experience God's peace, which exceeds anything we can understand" (Phil. 4:6–7).

Second, we must prevent planning from diminishing the value of the gifts God has already entrusted to our ministry. "Think about things that are excellent and worthy of praise. . . . I know how to live on almost nothing or with everything. I have learned the secret of living in every situation, whether it is with a full stomach or empty, with plenty or little. For I can do everything through Christ, who gives me strength" (Phil. 4:8, 12–13).

4. Destination Planning Delays Decisions, Creates Tension, Limits Dialogue, and Sets Unrealistic Expectations

A sister Christian university and Belhaven had the same problem, and we set out to solve it on nearly the same day. My university addressed the need by examining what opportunities we saw that might address the issue, while the other school appointed a traditional planning committee. We had a solution in forty-five days, and they came to a solution fifteen months later. Ours worked and still is in effect today. But, unfortunately, they had to go back to the drawing board after four years and do it all over again.

Traditional planning delays decisions to the point that the solutions are often partially irrelevant by the time they are settled. The protracted process most often adds to the tension because everything comes to a halt waiting for the planning group to finish their work. Discussion is limited because we seek to contain all dialogue within the cone of confidentiality required of the planning team.

Worst of all, it creates short-lived hope because imagined projections of the future can never live up to reality. I've built lots of buildings over the years, but I learned after the first half-dozen never to commission an architectural rendering of the building. First, those drawings are very costly, but more importantly, they are even more costly to morale because no building could look as good as the perfectly drawn architect's rendering.

> TRADITIONAL PLANNING CREATES THE FANTASY OF AN UNREALISTIC FUTURE IN WHICH ALL NEEDS ARE FULLY MET, WHILE CHALLENGES AND TENSIONS EVAPORATE. IF EVALUATED IN THE HARSH LIGHT OF DAY, PLANNING NEARLY ALWAYS DISAPPOINTS BECAUSE THE ROUGH EDGES OF REALITY CAN NEVER LIVE UP TO THE FULFILLMENT OF AN IMAGINER'S DRAWING.

5. Destination Planning Is Somewhat Silly in That It Nearly Always Focuses Attention on Contrived Numbers

Why would your goals be met in the year 2030, instead of 2029 or 2031? Why are our financial needs for a project nearly always set at $1 million, $5 million, or $10 million, or another even number, instead of a specific need? Why are our efforts for evangelistic reach always in round numbers that end with at least three zeros, as are our projections for the crowd invited to a major gathering?

Goals stated in bold round numbers are not a hallmark of planning—that's marketing. It is okay for messaging, if that's the easiest way to communicate the vision to your constituency. But don't confuse bold round numbers with meaningful plans.

I'm convinced that leaders spend more time cleaning up from the complications sparked by traditional planning than by what they might accomplish in desiring to move their ministry forward. While sailing is challenging, it doesn't leave behind the pollution that taints the waters we navigate.

Expecting Opportunities

About four years into my university's experiment in applying this developing idea of Opportunity Leadership, I was privileged to present the sailboat versus powerboat concept as part of my keynote address at the 2004 Forum for World Evangelization sponsored by the Lausanne Movement. One of those in attendance was my friend Rob Martin, the director of a large and influential foundation. He became fascinated by this idea and subsequently wrote about our Thailand discussions in his book, *When Money Goes on Mission: Fundraising and Giving in the 21st Century.*[1]

After the conference, Rob asked if he could bring a dozen leaders to Jackson to spend three days examining how Opportunity Leadership works in practice. It was a treat to host his friends from around the world, and we had engaging iron-sharpening-iron discussions during those days. Their questions and probing helped push forward my thinking about how this unique approach to preparing for the future is lived out.

The last evening of that time together created a breakthrough moment for me in my understanding of why abandoning powerboats in favor of sailboats works so remarkably. It was late in the evening, and we'd been going all day. The conversation had gotten to that point where everything to be said had been said, and the room was becoming still and quiet.

Finally, breaking the silence, but in a hushed and reverent tone, a ministry leader from South America looked at me and summarized it all, insightfully pronouncing, "You really *expect* God to bring you opportunities, don't you?"

That was it! It had never really hit me that bluntly before—but yes, we had shifted our focus from looking for opportunities to expecting the Lord will bring them to us. And since that day, I've never looked any other direction than where the wind of God is blowing.

> AFTER MANY YEARS OF LIVING OUT OPPORTUNITY LEADERSHIP, I'LL OFTEN SIT IN MY OFFICE NEAR THE START OF AN ACADEMIC YEAR AND REFLECTIVELY ASK, "I WONDER WHAT I'LL DO THIS YEAR?" BECAUSE I OFTEN DON'T KNOW.

Now, after many years of living out Opportunity Leadership, I'll often sit in my office near the start of a school year and reflectively ask, "I wonder what I'll do this year?" Because I often don't know. Most of the new priorities that fill my agenda as I write this were not even on my radar a year ago—that is how dramatically the wind of God will blow when we get out of our powerboats.

The wind of God is always refreshing on the deck of a sailboat. But we need to be prepared to respond to His leading toward new destinations—or to patiently wait for the breeze to pick up again.

Chapter 5

Making the Transition to Opportunity Leadership

The predictable uncertainty triggered by organizational change, for good or bad, always generates tension from the biggest to smallest modifications. To experience in a microcosm the predictable dynamics of change, simply move the shared office copy machine to a new location.

- A loss of control is inherent in change because patterns of routine must be realigned.

  The newly moved copy machine is no longer convenient for some employees, but now, those with offices near the new device don't like the hallway's noise.

- Change creates more work for everyone.

  With the copy machine moved, some employees must walk further, and others are now being interrupted when the chatter of congregating coworkers infiltrates their space.

- Past resentments come to the surface during times of change.

  Rumors surmise that those closest to the relocated copy machine get what they want only because they frequently complain about it the loudest.

- During times of change, anxiety rises as employees wait in anticipation for other shoes to drop.

  Could moving a copy machine be preparation for downsizing or expansion, replacing jobs with more technology, or a leadership reorganization?

Even the best people tend to become inwardly fearful, aggressive, and judgmental in times of change, and the difficult employees show those traits outwardly. Having watched hundreds of ministries cope with change-triggered tension, I am convinced that most people would rather live in mediocrity than grapple with a change that pushes them into uncertainty.

Elevating from the apparent simplicity of moving a copy machine to the certain complexity of shifting the entire focus of your planning model to Opportunity Leadership, you must be purposeful, prepared, patient, and personal to bring a ministry through this enormous revolution. If the transition is too abrupt, it will not be long before those under your care raise the alarm and question your ability and mission commitment.

One-of-a-Kind Transition

There is no predictable and universal multi-step formula to shift seamlessly from one leadership model to the other. Those whiteboard-designed task charts are being left behind with the old model of traditional planning. Instead, each ministry begins this transition at their unique position along the planning spectrum—clenched-grip control at one end, all the way to a relaxed open palm at the other. From here, your conversion must factor in your unique blend of distinctives, including your ministry's mission and priorities, leadership style and experience, and key employees' expertise coupled with your bench strength, organizational size/scope, and resources, plus the board's structure and level of engagement.

To launch this shift:

1. Begin assuring that the senior leadership team understands the primary concepts driving each of the two planning models.

2. Evaluate your gifting and leadership methods, considering the six talents of Opportunity Leaders.

3. Don't go any further until you can begin to "see, feel, and own it," not just study it.

Once those concepts are internalized, you are ready to thoughtfully broaden the discussion to pockets of stakeholders, focusing on those who easily resonate with the new vision. Don't worry too much about the resisters just yet. Provide assurance all along the way that this is not an all-or-nothing switch. This allows them to embrace the ideas that feel most accessible in your setting. As a little bit of buy-in begins to take hold, these stakeholders will be drawn to Opportunity Leadership as they see how capturing small opportunities can produce visible results. There is nothing like a little success to bring people along.

After these initial steps, you'll be amazed as unexpected opportunities begin to multiply and expand, giving you handles for leading your ministry through this change. Then, having waited patiently for a little momentum to build and some demonstrations of success that you can tout, broaden your vision to equip and empower people to break free from the confines of structured planning and begin to look for opportunities. And most importantly, infuse your ministry with a shared theological understanding that enables an ever-widening circle of employees, stakeholders, and donors to embrace the Opportunity Leadership model operationally.

Inner Circle
Education

Theologial
Commitment

Six Talents Assessment

Early Adopter
Stakeholders

Small Successes

Broader Buy-In

Breaking Free From
Traditional Planning

Here is a key: the Opportunity Leadership model will first take root internally during the early stages of this switch. Do not expect this transition to transform on your schedule and to your destination. Instead, focus on day one, as you would in the launch of a traditional planning model. Your attention should be laser-trained to recognize God-given opportunities that crack open new doors close to home as you lead your ministry into this new outlook. Building trust by capturing opportunities in your inner circle prepares the way to venture out. From the very beginning, expect God to bring you opportunities. They will come.

> EXPECT GOD TO BRING YOU OPPORTUNITIES. THEY WILL COME.

This won't be an easy transition, and it will take time. As you prepare for this journey, my strongest warning is to be ready for the overwhelming temptation to revert to traditional planning as soon as the going gets tough. Your sketchy roadmap may look simple on paper. The journey will be arduous, but it will also be well worth it.

Our Theology Sets It in Motion

Billy Graham's sister, Jean Ford, has been a dear friend for years. I've had the joy of chairing the board of Leighton Ford Ministries and working closely with Jean and her husband Leighton through the Lausanne Movement. By empowering a younger generation of evangelism leaders, their reach has been enormous, even though their ministry focus was grounded in tragedy. Their gifted and God-honoring twenty-one-year-old son, Sandy, died during heart surgery. The story of losing their son during his college years is overwhelming to grasp, but even more breathtaking is Jean's eternal perspective on their tragedy.

One afternoon on their back porch in North Carolina, my wife MaryLou and I were visiting with Jean and talking about God's leading in every aspect of life. During that conversation, Jean shared one of the most profound insights that tested my theological core. Reflecting on their son Sandy's early death, she declared, "You have to decide, either God is sovereign in everything, or He's not at all. There is no middle ground."

Of course, I trust God completely—and you do too. But while it is so easy to be confident that God is sovereign in all, it is so hard to let go of our need to control and faithfully live out our theology. Why do we keep projecting God's destinations for our ministry if we want our Lord to lead us to His best outcome? Has God delegated to us the decisions about our ministry's future?

Is a "no" from God as good as a "yes"? Do we ever celebrate when what we worked for doesn't come about because God blocked it? Opportunity Leadership demands a complete and unwavering dependency on the sovereignty of God—both professionally and personally.

Early in my ministry life, my father wisely advised, "Never get your heart set on one specific job." He was right because I've seen scores of great leaders drained of their usefulness when a position for which they longed did not come their way. So I always resisted that temptation. That is except for one time when I was interviewing for the presidency of the American Bible Society (ABS) in New York City, one of the oldest and most significant ministries in the country. I love their global reach and pure focus on Scripture. It was a job I really wanted.

After several rounds of interviews and discussions, the search process worked its way down to two finalists. I was excited to be considered for the ABS presidency because it demanded all the gifting that best suited my experience. Their global reach mirrored my commitment to world evangelism, and the educational component of ABS fitted a university president. Besides all of that, they had a large endowment, a vast constituency, and it would have meant living in the most exciting city in the world.

> OPPORTUNITY LEADERSHIP DEMANDS A COMPLETE AND UNWAVERING DEPENDENCY ON THE SOVEREIGNTY OF GOD—BOTH PROFESSIONALLY AND PERSONALLY.

On the morning of the final interview, I was having breakfast alone at a window table in the top floor dining room of the New York Athletic Club overlooking Central Park. Thinking about living in New York and praying for wisdom to communicate my vision for ABS, I asked God to grant my desire to have the privilege of leading this significant work.

Thankfully, the interview could not have gone better, and the whispers I received gave an assurance that the offer of the presidency would be coming my way. I was thrilled.

Two days later, the executive search firm called late in the day as I was driving home from my campus office in Mississippi. I pulled over to concentrate as I was ready to hear the good news. But, instead, I was told the board selected the other finalist. He had accepted, and a reimbursement check for my trip to New York was in the mail. That was it—and I was devastated.

God had said no, and the last thing I was ready to do was to celebrate. Tears of disappointment filled my eyes, and sadness filled my heart. I thought this was the role which God had been preparing for me all my life.

But God's plans are never wrong.

Two years after our family would have moved to New York City to lead a ministry where money was never a problem, the stock market crashed, and their endowment lost half its value. ABS laid off a large segment of their staff, and the rest took salary cuts. They began some tough years that saw the new president resigning far before he had planned.

More importantly, it was almost immediately after ABS turned me down that God ignited a firestorm of remarkable open-door opportunities at Belhaven University, where I continued as president. Our enrollment doubled, we built many new buildings, added new academic programs, and dramatically expanded our reach, including internationally. God's "no" was far better than His "yes" to my plan. I realized that I was already in the role God had been preparing for me all of my life.

God has our future planned—both personally and professionally. Opportunity Leadership has proven that rather than forcing square pegs into round holes because we are convinced of God's direction for us, we can be both theologically and emotionally relaxed in the assurance our best future will be 100 percent guided by God-given opportunities. Both our actions and our spirit must be anchored to this theological bedrock.

If you trust God but hold tightly to an agenda, Opportunity Leadership won't work. If you trust God but you're overly anxious about what the future may or may not bring, then Opportunity Leadership will become a confusing mess.

As Jean Ford so pithily articulated, "God is either sovereign, or He's not." Focusing your ministry's future on opportunities rather than conference-table planning begins at the foot of the cross. If we don't make a theological commitment that shapes the core of our leadership ethos, the rest won't matter.

> FOCUSING YOUR MINISTRY'S FUTURE ON OPPORTUNITIES RATHER THAN CONFERENCE-TABLE PLANNING BEGINS AT THE FOOT OF THE CROSS. IF WE DON'T MAKE A THEOLOGICAL COMMITMENT THAT SHAPES THE CORE OF OUR LEADERSHIP ETHOS, THE REST WON'T MATTER.

This thorough embracing of God's sovereignty is the big hurdle to Opportunity Leadership. If you cross this bridge without reservation, the next steps become exciting, fun, and fulfilling. But if you decide it is impossible to switch from a traditional planning model and you're ready to put this book on the shelf, the Lord still loves you and will honor your work. But I believe you'll be capturing only a limited portion of what He could do through your ministry until you let go of your plans and become focused on His opportunities.

Begin Watching for Opportunities As You Let Go of Planning

The axis of Opportunity Leadership takes root by developing an organizational culture of expectancy with both processes and people equipped to move with speed at critical junctures. But that culture needs to be equally comfortable in patiently waiting for those opportune moments to appear. A stark look at the differences in organizational culture brings into focus the uniqueness of this new outlook, in contrast to a ministry framed around traditional planning.

Eleven ministry culture characteristics highlight the distinctions between traditional planning and Opportunity Leadership. This chart is not offered as a scorecard to identify where your ministry currently falls on the spectrum of planning. Still, it might provide an interesting insight to circle each of the chart's characteristics that best describes your ministry's culture. For each ministry culture characteristic, force a choice between one column or the other.

MINISTRY CULTURE CHARACTERISTIC	TRADITIONAL PLANNING	OPPORTUNITY LEADERSHIP
Initial Reaction	Probably NO	Probably YES
Future Outlook	Cautious and Analytical	Confident and Expectant
Ministry Boundaries	History and Structures	Mission and Strengths
Biblical Image	Nehemiah's Wall	Lilies of the Field
Decision Process	Measured and Concrete	Responsive and Fluid
Team Characteristics	Expertise and Focus	Generalists and Nimble
Leadership Agenda	Methodical and Inclusive	Aggressive and Empowering
Pace of Change	Predictive and Deliberate	Patient and Ambiguous
Board Focus	Definition and Authority	Guidelines and Trust
Communications	Decisions and Achievements	Reflections and Evolvement
Risk of Failure	Embarrassing	Tolerable

The coming chapters will compare, contrast, and interweave these eleven cultural characteristics. But in summary, those embracing Opportunity Leadership's ministry culture find it free-flowing, less structured, mission-guided, quick-paced, and enormously adventurous. In contrast, traditional planning culture is measured, deliberative, regulated, systematized, and conservative.

Having had years of experience in both models, the core difference may be most profoundly characterized by the first of these eleven characteristics: Initial Reaction. Opportunity Leaders are open to nearly any new idea and don't say "no" to an idea until they must. For them, one meeting will often set the gears in motion leading to an entirely new venture. Traditional planning leaders usually start with caution, and only warm to new ideas after reflecting and broadening their sphere of consideration because they are most comfortable with multiple discussions between each step in their evaluation process.

Opportunity Leadership may not be the ideal fit for every ministry leader, but for those who fully embrace it, there is freedom and joy in their responsibility. They run to keep up with God's new directions, rather than wrestle the organizational practices that inhibit innovation and responsiveness.

With these contrasts in mind, it is time to move from the panorama view to the ground level of Opportunity Leadership by exploring six talents of these leaders and six tendencies of their ministries.

Part 2

6 TALENTS OF OPPORTUNITY LEADERS

If you've been a team-sport athlete, you understand that each player must hone their skills before the team can work together successfully. It is not enough to theoretically comprehend how to dribble with either hand, pass the ball, or shoot jump shots in basketball. Those skills need to be purposefully nurtured and practiced individually over and over again before the team ever attempts to play together.

This section addresses the six talents you must tenaciously cultivate as an Opportunity Leader to help your team work effectively in this new model. These are the fundamentals—dribbling, passing, and shooting. And in the following section, we'll examine the six tendencies that will bring fulfillment and success to Opportunity Leadership-driven ministries.

Because Opportunity Leadership demands a new level of complete dependency and trust in God to provide opportunities, spiritual leadership becomes as essential as organizational operations to guide a ministry in this model. Both are critical and need to become one-and-the-same as Opportunity Leaders develop skills and experience. I would challenge you to look for ways to build a new level of interconnectedness between leadership's operational and spiritual dimensions.

As you focus on these new talents, don't leave behind those leadership best practices you've already learned. The full litany of typical leadership skills is just as crucial to ministry leaders working within the Opportunity Leadership model as it is to leaders focused on traditional planning. These include qualities such as approachability, listening, empowering, motivating, and the list goes on. But to capture opportunities, you will need to add to your strengths the following six talents that will take you beyond the typical *Harvard Business Review* inventory of leadership attributes.

Chapter 6

Leading Without a Plan Is the Plan

A s a Fortune 400 CEO enters the ballroom of a New York City hotel and strides confidently to the podium to begin the annual stockholders meeting, a hush falls over the crowd of investors, brokers, journalists, and competitors. Anticipation has been building to unveil a plan for the coming year, as billions of dollars are at stake depending on the viability of the soon-to-be-announced future objectives.

Rumors speculate possible competitor take-overs, new product lines, or geographic market advances because the CEO has a history of projecting bold and measurable objectives. Simultaneously, the stock price, market share, and company wages have lagged for years because the goals are rarely achieved, even though each annual announcement creates an air of excitement, with supporters believing "this could be the turning point" toward a break-out future.

"Ladies and gentlemen," the CEO begins, "this year is going to be different. I don't have on the screen my usual PowerPoint presentation outlining new goals for the year ahead. I know you're expecting that, but based on what I'm about to say, I think you'll be even more excited about our future as a company.

"This year, I want to speak to you transparently. By this time next year, I don't know if we'll have more customers or fewer, but I do know we want to serve well the ones we have. Projecting a year ahead, I don't know if we'll add staff or need to trim positions—that will depend on how our focus takes shape plus factors beyond our control. And looking into the future, I don't know what products we might roll out, although some interesting ideas are churning up as we look to capture opportunities.

"Capturing opportunities is the plan for the coming year, and we don't need a plan beyond waiting for the right opportunities to develop. I don't know where we will be as a company a year from now, but I will tell you what I know for sure: the best plans we could come up with around conference tables pale in comparison to the plan God has for us. So we're going to release control of our future to God's leading, and trust Him to bring us the right opportunities fitting with the strengths of our team and correlating best with our mission."

Within minutes of the first tweets leaving the room, the stock price plummets and key employees resign. The board calls an emergency session to appoint a new CEO because it is evident that the current one cannot lead.

Comprehensive bold measurable plans that articulate new destinations are what the world expects. But kingdom work is not of the world. It is not even close.

Upside-Down Kingdom Leadership

Why is it that in Christian leadership we continue to operate as if we are in a secular world? Of course, we need to use the best tools and experience of the broader leadership arena, but kingdom work is very different.

The ways of God are not the ways of the world, but we have become relentless in forcing the world's methods into God's kingdom structure. It doesn't work. While it is appropriate to lay out mission, policy, or principle ideals, it is when those dreams morph into projected hard results that the bottom falls out. And then we are surprised when our lofty planning goals come up far short of the envisioned future. We shouldn't be.

What if we started with God's way first and then co-opted applicable leadership principles into a kingdom perspective, instead of starting with the secular framework and asking God to bless it? Kingdom practices are nearly always upside down from how the world operates. Donald Kraybill's wonderful book, *The Upside-Down Kingdom*, captures this concept with this thesis: ". . . the kingdom of God points to an inverted, upside-down way of life that challenges the prevailing social order."[1] Why should leadership be any different?

Anticipating well-defined future destinations may work in the secular world (although I would argue it doesn't work all that well there either). Their constituency expects structured planning, and frankly, those leaders essentially don't have a choice. In the political, business, educational, sports, and even non-profit arenas (any arena other than kingdom work), constituencies won't stand for a leader who doesn't craft and articulate bold future objectives. Have you ever seen a politician even come close to achieving the perfection of their envisioned objectives during an election campaign? Of course not! But the way our culture is programmed, attempting to lead without a plan that details the future won't get you elected to a political office.

Just like all aspects of our Christian life, when secular ideas

> GOD WILL USE THE INSPIRATION, WISDOM, INTUITION, AND EXPERIENCE OF YOU AND OTHERS TO REVEAL HIS DIRECTION. HE WILL USE UNEXPECTED CONVERSATIONS, NEW FRIENDSHIPS, AND "CHANCE" ENCOUNTERS, ALONG WITH CHANGING CIRCUMSTANCES. ALL OF THESE COULD TRIGGER SURPRISES YOU NEVER IMAGINED.

bombard the biblical distinctiveness of our leadership long enough, the world's way becomes acceptable. Ministry leadership concepts have become so deeply meshed with secular leadership ideas that we dutifully follow their pattern without even realizing who we are NOT following. But kingdom work is an arena where we can take hold of both the courage and obligation to completely trust God for a different way to order our plans and do things upside-down from the world's approach.

Jesus didn't mirror the normative practices of organizational leadership in ancient Israel:

- He was inclusive rather than hierarchical.
- He allowed interruptions rather than schedules to most often guide His activities.
- He "hired staff" without the articulation of a plan, destination, or layered structure.

And getting further into the weeds to demonstrate His unorthodox approach to leadership, Jesus sent the most unlikely character, John the Baptist, to announce His coming. John was the worst public relations guy you could ever hire if you wanted a warm introduction. You and I would both get fired for making that hire.

From the very beginning, Jesus demonstrated that kingdom leadership was different—not just a little bit different, but totally different. Kingdom work was going to make it possible that "valleys will be filled, and the mountains and hills made level. The curves will be straightened, and the rough places made smooth" (Luke 3:5). Throughout His public ministry, Jesus made it clear that what you expect is not what will be. His model of leadership was just as "upside-down" as most everything else He did.

Let me take a moment to be ultra-clear so that your effort to embrace Opportunity Leadership won't be thwarted by the objections of others who have bought into the full secular model. I strongly believe in learning from the best of leadership in the secular world, and I'm not advocating ignoring those concepts. But if we dig deeper, even a little bit of leadership study reveals that some of the best business practices are based on biblical ideals.

To be more specific, the well-researched and precisely articulated work of Jim Collins in his milestone book, *Good to Great*, is jam-packed with solid biblically-based leadership principles. His identification of Level 5 leaders would appear to be rooted in Galatians 5:22–23 (fruit of the Spirit) if we didn't know it came from pure academic research:

- "Level 5 leaders are a study in duality: modest and willful, humble and fearless."[2]

- "Level 5 leaders channel their ego needs away from themselves and into the larger goal of building a great company. It's not that Level 5 leaders have no ego or self-interest. Indeed, they are incredibly ambitious—*but their ambition is first and foremost for the institution, not themselves.*"[3]

- "Those who worked with or wrote about the good-to-great leader continually used words like *quiet, humble, modest, reserved, shy, gracious, mild-mannered, self-effacing, understated, did not believe his own clippings;* and so forth."[4]

- "Every good-to-great transition in our research began with a Level 5 leader who motivated the enterprise more with inspired standards than inspiring personality."[5]

Don't discard what you've learned about leadership as you move into Opportunity Leadership. Instead, hold onto the best of what we've all absorbed as planners, and shift those skills into a new level of trusting God for direction and being responsive to both strong gales and gentle breezes as the wind of God blows.

The Lord won't deliver every new opportunity to your doorstep in a package as if ordered online. He will use the inspiration, wisdom, intuition, and experience of you and others to reveal His direction. He will use unexpected conversations, new friendships, and "chance" encounters, along with changing circumstances. All of these could trigger surprises you never imagined. But using leadership tools to capture God-given destinations is very different from a determined effort that powers toward the goals of a strategic plan, no matter which way the wind of God is blowing.

How It Works in Real Time

An example with clear takeaways may be helpful to demonstrate how this works at a practical level.

More than a dozen years ago, a close friend introduced me to his friend. That new friend was also in the education world, and we began to connect every year or so to compare notes about innovative ideas.

A decade later, that second friend introduced me to his business-connected friend. And a year later, those two friends together introduced me to their business-linked friend (five degrees of separation) that enabled our university to develop one of the most dynamic MBA programs in all of Christian higher education.

Opportunity Leadership Takeaway: *All friendships matter in leadership. Never burn a bridge because you don't know what opportunity could be on the other side.*

The last friend in that chain is Michael Moe, author of *Finding the Next Starbucks* and president of Global Silicon Valley. *The Wall Street Journal* named him one of the most influential power-players for start-up companies working in education. He has developed a track record of success by being on the ground floor of Coursera, Chegg, Pluralsight, 2U, and CourseHero, among others.

Michael has been pouring his life into young entrepreneurs

through a significant annual conference he holds in partnership with one of America's most influential flagship public universities.

But he had been looking for a way to take his entrepreneurship teaching to a deeper level. My friends envisioned with Michael an MBA degree that would teach entrepreneurship at a practical and personal level. And, all three being strong Christians, they wanted biblical principles baked into the curriculum.

> ALL FRIENDSHIPS MATTER IN LEADERSHIP. NEVER BURN A BRIDGE BECAUSE YOU DON'T KNOW WHAT OPPORTUNITY COULD BE ON THE OTHER SIDE.

Unlike any other MBA in America, this program would allow every assignment in the entire course of study to be designed around each student's future business. The vision was to recruit students who dream of starting a specific business—tech company, restaurant, delivery service, etc.—and the course projects would be sculptured around their business, enabling them to graduate with a fully developed plan for their new venture.

Opportunity Leadership Takeaway: *Ideas that are outside your normal comfort zone shouldn't be discarded before consideration. But if there is not some meaningful connection to your core strengths, then you're probably chasing rainbows and not capturing opportunities.*

After exploring the concept with several high-profile universities and quickly running into their standard bureaucratic barriers, my friends suggested this Entrepreneurship MBA might fit well with Belhaven as a fully online degree. When I received the first phone call, I thought it was one of the most exciting ideas I'd ever heard.

But as much as I was inspired, I saw a multitude of problems that would have to be solved:

- Would our faculty allow someone outside our sphere to be deeply involved in curriculum writing?

- What would the accreditors think of such a practical degree based on a student's specific business plan?

- Michael was deeply connected in China and wanted us to teach in Mandarin as well, but could we support a global reach?

- How could we find a marketing partner that would allow us to scale quickly?

- How are all the key entities financially incentivized to make the program grow?

- How much infrastructure staff would the program require, and did we have the team strength to pull it off?

- Would this new MBA cannibalize enrollment from our regular corporate-focused MBA?

That list of questions went on and on.

Opportunity Leadership Takeaway: *Opportunity Leaders learn through experience not to get hung up on the questions and concerns until you determine if the big idea is even possible. Keep saying "yes" until you are forced to say "no."*

OPPORTUNITY LEADERS LEARN THROUGH EXPERIENCE NOT TO GET HUNG UP ON THE QUESTIONS AND CONCERNS UNTIL YOU DETERMINE IF THE BIG IDEA IS EVEN POSSIBLE. KEEP SAYING "YES" UNTIL YOU ARE FORCED TO SAY "NO."

Michael had his choice narrowed down to one of America's most wealthy and highly-ranked universities or to establish the degree with Belhaven University. Any way you slice that decision, the obvious choice was not us, and I was okay with that because I knew this would be a gigantic project filled with challenges. We had to be assured this was God's direction because when the tough obstacles emerged, we needed to have confidence that we were following the will of the Lord.

Opportunity Leadership Takeaway: *If consideration of an opportunity is only practical and not spiritual, you're likely to make a mistake. The only objective is to find God's direction because that answer will always be perfect in the long run.*

Michael was just as deeply committed as we were to being responsive to the wind of God. The decision boiled down to two factors:

1. If he developed the degree with Belhaven, Michael could be deeply engaged in writing the curriculum versus the highly structured wealthy school, whose faculty were not about to give up their authority over the curriculum.

2. If the degree were developed with the premier university, it would be accessible only to the wealthy and academically gifted versus our desire to offer the degree in an approachable format and at an affordable price. And the big bonus was our shared desire to teach entrepreneurship based on biblical values.

Opportunity Leadership Takeaway: *I didn't push for the idea to be developed with us instead of an elite university, while at the same time doing all I could to accommodate the idea of moving forward with us. That balance is the key, and you'll know it when you hit it.*

Michael went with us, and we eventually worked out all the questions and challenges to launch the program in the fall of 2020.

Just Enough Light for the Next Steps

Hopefully, you're ready to move to a higher level of leading the kingdom way, grounded in trusting God for opportunities rather than creating plans. That's great, but it's not that simple.

"It's inspiring you would trust God that much," will be the response of your board or inner circle, "but what's the *real plan* for leading without a plan?" After hearing your reiteration, emphasizing that "the plan is that there is no plan," they may follow by asking, "Okay, I'm ready to trust God for our future with you, *but really*, just tell me where are we headed?"

Emphasizing that you don't know what the future will look like will frustrate them, even though it is the biblical model of Abraham, David, and Peter. Your stakeholders will be thrilled with the theological commitment of Opportunity Leadership, but helping them accept the practical side will take time. Your steadfast commitment to this new model must be unwavering.

Those around you will need assurance this is not Lewis Carroll's *Alice's Adventures in Wonderland*, with Alice asking the Cheshire Cat for direction:

> "Would you tell me, please, which way I ought to go from here?"
> "That depends a good deal on where you want to get to," said the Cat.
> "I don't much care where—" said Alice.
> "Then it doesn't matter which way you go," said the Cat.[6]

With Opportunity Leadership, we know *exactly* where we are going. We are going where God guides us, and we trust Him for that direction rather than praying the map we created is accurate. But, of course, if you don't expect God to bring you opportunities, then you're as aimless as the Cheshire Cat.

With some practice and success, you will become comfortable and confident that the plan is not to have a plan. And along with that pledge, you will hone your ability to articulate that understanding to others to get their buy-in, or at least buy enough time—before they fire you—to show that it works in kingdom business.

There is no "Plan B" in Opportunity Leadership. Do not always be thinking that if God doesn't bring you opportunities, you'll still have time to develop a plan. No, if the wind of God doesn't blow, you'll learn just to wait.

Remember, either God is sovereign or He's not. Why wouldn't the Lord bring you the right ministry opportunities? Doesn't He want more ministry, not less? God is not holding you back. Rather, it is your cumbersome planning model that is holding Him back from fully utilizing your ministry. If you're prepared to be a good steward of new ministry opportunities, you can completely trust that God will bring them to you.

The internal and external questioning you'll experience as you wade in the shallow end of Opportunity Leadership will mostly revolve around previously discussed stakeholder expectations and the sometimes blurred line between operational planning and destination planning. But, with time and consistency, you can handle those.

There is one other hurdle to address, though. It is the fear of not being able to see what the future will bring. Down deep, could this be why we are so attached to traditional planning? Laying out goals for the coming few years gives us a false sense of control over an unknown future. If we project destinations, even if those goals are not met, that look over the horizon makes us feel more secure than staring into the darkness of the unknown.

Ralph Waldo Emerson wrote, "We are never tired, so long as we can see far enough."[7] Organizations get tired easily. Even the most fulfilling of ministry can become a grind. The burnout among pastors and ministry leaders is far too high, partly due to their inability to see the light at the end of the tunnel.

There is no doubt that traditional

> THERE IS NO "PLAN B" IN OPPORTUNITY LEADERSHIP. DO NOT ALWAYS BE THINKING THAT IF GOD DOESN'T BRING YOU OPPORTUNITIES, YOU'LL STILL HAVE TIME TO DEVELOP A PLAN. NO, IF THE WIND OF GOD DOESN'T BLOW, YOU'LL LEARN JUST TO WAIT.

planning brings a brief relief that lifts, or at least puts on hold, the pressure, intensity, confusion, or criticism that comes with ministry work. As discussed earlier, the process of planning hits the pause button, and promising a brighter future releases the pressure—that is, until that new future doesn't come about. Then, what was before comes roaring back with even more intensity.

Teach yourself and others that NOT being able to see the future is one of God's greatest gifts to us. In providing just enough light for the next steps, rather than illuminating the entire journey, God has been gracious to give us time, experience, and wisdom to be ready to handle what is to come.

If you have been in ministry for a while, how would you have faced the future if you'd known from the beginning everything the journey would demand of you? I know that in my case, I'm not sure I would have said yes if the search committee called to invite me to be Belhaven's next president and added, "Along with everything else, we will need you to lead the school through a hurricane, a couple of major recessions, a historic building falling down, and a crippling pandemic that may risk the future of the entire institution."

When we look back in our lives, we see how gracious God has been not to give us enough light for the entire journey, but instead, always provide just enough light for the next few steps. Basking in the light we have been given, without expecting the entire pathway to be illuminated, is fundamental to capturing opportunities.

As you develop your talents as an Opportunity Leader, there will be times when you have no clue what comes next, and other times you will have too many good choices to prioritize. If you become comfortable with just enough light for the next steps, this will be an incredible journey.

Chapter 7

Staying in Your Lane

W alking away from the best deal I could have ever imagined was easy—sort of. But I did so with confidence that God is always leading us to the right opportunities and blocking the wrong ones.

My board chair and I had flown to a hub airport to meet in a terminal conference room with our counterparts from a sister college. The meeting was to be the culmination of six months of discussion, analysis, and negotiation. Responding to their request, we would absorb their institution into ours.

I deeply admired the courage of their president, who had initiated the exploration of this possibility. Reading the projected downward trends for Christian higher education, he called when their institution was not desperate and had enough strengths that we could meld their advantages into Belhaven to make this an attractive collaboration. Wisely, he didn't want to wait until there was nothing left in the cupboards before seeking a partnership.

They had a residential campus in an attractive location, where we would continue to run the institution as a unique and different experience from our primary campus. Their school had enjoyed a long history of academic success and had gained distinction within their supporting denomination. Most immediately attractive to us, they had established branch campuses in significant markets of the southeastern section of the United States, including complementary cities to our five other branch campuses across the region.

They were of our same theological focus, had a deep bench of potential donors, and offered some academic programs that we could not provide at our limited-space campus in Jackson, Mississippi. We knew and liked their people, and our faculty and staff were supportive of the idea. If the acquisition went through, our total enrollment would grow by a third overnight.

We had turned their institution inside out to examine it in detail, and although it required some significant hard work to realign priorities and costs, we believed it was fixable. It wouldn't be easy, but the long-term outcome could be a big win-win for all involved.

It seemed like the perfect fit. It wasn't.

Mission Fit Is Not about Mission Statements

As we considered absorbing the other institution, the problem wasn't money, facilities, programs, or expertise when we got down to brass tacks. What brought the opportunity to a screeching halt was discovering a misalignment of mission-implementation priorities and style that would have been the root of endless conflicts had we gone ahead. I saw it clearly on the plane ride home, but why hadn't we seen it earlier?

When examining any new opportunity, there is a tendency to focus on the logistics rather than the calling. Obviously, none of us would consider an extension into an arena that wasn't closely aligned with our central mission. It is quick and easy to say no to opportunities far outside our mission and expertise sphere.

But when we contemplated the prospect of teaming with an entity traveling alongside us in the next lane, we assumed this would be a strong match because they were headed where we wanted to go. We were reminded that, yes, mission direction is primary, but if it requires changing lanes, we need to be careful and not gloss over the hard questions to scrutinize mission congruence.

In my example, the finance, logistics, and primary assets all lined up. The other school's needs meshed well with our ability to dissect and rebuild programs and administrative functions, expand markets, introduce new services, and enhance operations by scaling.

And, because we'd been traveling alongside them in the next lane over for a long time, we didn't slow down to consider mission fit questions. We were not fearful of drifting out of our lane because we assumed our lanes would smoothly merge. Our schools shared a common denominational heritage, long-term friendships with some of their key leadership, and evident interconnectedness in our overarching mission of Christian higher education. We presumed the alignment was an easy match on both sides, so neither institution drilled down past the surface level of mission fit.

As I've studied other ministries that have inherited problems while capturing opportunities, I've discovered it's a common experience to make assumptions about mission fit without asking the tough questions. Like driving an automobile, we have a blind spot when changing lanes. Unless we keep our eye on the warning light, what we expect will be an easy shift could lead to disaster.

> SOMETIMES HEARING GOD'S "NO" ABOUT A NEW OPPORTUNITY MAY LEAD US BACK TO OUR ROOTS.

In ministry, each of us has a distinct mission that drives us, coupled with a unique history that has shaped that mission. To articulate it internally and externally, we periodically recraft it and wordsmith our mission summary, so each phrase has a purpose. We test it with our constituency and adopt it with fanfare. We ask our teams to memorize the summary sentence, we publish it in our materials, and most importantly, we expect to be piloted by that mission statement in all we do.

This formal document is the starting point of defining our

mission, but it is far from the ending point. In practice, missions are not words on paper but are instead lived out in relationships, budgets, structures, operational style, decisions, marketing, priorities, and various other components. A mission statement may be a roadmap for the general direction a ministry is headed. Still it doesn't usually stipulate the specific route, and it surely isn't an indicator of the subtleties of the most fitting lane.

Back to my example, please understand there wasn't anything "wrong" with the mission of the other college. If you put their mission statement and ours side by side and took the names off, you might have trouble telling them apart. That was the problem. We were driving next to each other on the primary issues, but where mission gets lived out—in the day-to-day relationships, decisions, style, and outlook—our synchronous direction and speed almost kept us from examining the blind spot that could have triggered a serious accident if we were to change lanes.

Abandoning opportunities that don't easily mesh with your mission takes grit and courage (especially after you've invested months of work). But a willingness to "walk away" from the negotiating table is central to successful Opportunity Leadership.

Notably, one of the most rewarding moments of my years in leadership came as my board chair and I walked back to the gate to catch our flight home. He said, "We asked God to bring us opportunities, and if God blocks them, that's just as good." So true—but it's often easier to preach than to live.

Sometimes hearing God's "no" about a new opportunity may lead us back to our roots.

Ask New Mission Questions

Opportunities will come to you as you move away from traditional planning. The more you get into the rhythm of responding to them, the finer you will grind the understanding of your mission. As you do, this helps you to determine which projects match well and which to pass over. Understanding that distinctive, though, will take some time.

Unfortunately, most ministries are extremely weak in understanding and articulating their mission beyond the 10,000-foot view description. So I'd suggest that before you lead your ministry too far down the path of Opportunity Leadership, take a fresh look at how your mission gets lived out day-to-day, rather than limiting your analysis to the published mission statement. If we are to find a ministry's future in being responsive to opportunities rather than destination planning, we must pinpoint mission, strengths, and shortcomings.

As you become more successful in capturing opportunities and your reach expands in complexity, there will come many options that will tempt you to stray outside your central calling or push you beyond the boundaries of your strengths. You must know who you are and why you are called before you can consider expanding your reach. A fresh, deep dive into mission will enable your ministry to set informed boundaries based on mission and strengths before doors are opened to the whole new world of initiatives.

The critical distinction is that in traditional planning leadership, these boundaries are most often set by organizational policies, patterns, history, and resources—rather than a laser focus on mission, strengths, and gifts. Because these hierarchical organizational structures have imprisoned us for so long, too many ministries have been held back by tradition rather than viewing opportunities from the grass-roots level of mission implementation.

Every ministry is different, and only you and your stakeholders will be able to evaluate the distinctiveness of your mission. But to help in that process, I'd suggest several questions for consideration. This deeper dive into understanding how your mission gets lived out isn't a one-time process—although a retreat or other event accelerates discernment. Senior leadership needs to continually ask these kinds of questions and make adjustments as new insights are revealed and circumstances change:

1. What's the worst that would happen if your ministry closed a year from now?

   • Other than the employment complexities, specify what difference it would make.

2. What is the cost of failure of a project, program, or initiative?

   • Our new efforts often fall short because we have not understood the stakes of coming up short.

3. What does board governance tell you about the mission?

   • Boards hold ministries accountable for their mission and set policies that enable the mission to be achieved. Your agenda should reflect these priorities.

4. How do committees and meetings advance or limit mission fulfillment?

   • Most larger organizations have too many committees, and all-size ministries tie people down with too many meetings, which often stifle mission fulfillment rather than enhance it.

5. How would your mission shift if you lost a key person?

   • An irreplaceable gap in your calling with the loss of a key person indicates larger mission issues.

6. How do the lowest-paid people define your mission?

   • Every position in a ministry should be mission-driven— from top to bottom.

7. How do mid-tier employees live out your mission?

   • Senior leadership may challenge stakeholders to embrace an inspiring mission, but those on the front lines must implement it every day.

8. What aspects of the mission encouraged your newest employees/constituents to join with you?

   • A mission becomes too familiar over time, so learning what attracts new employees and constituents will help to prioritize mission objectives.

9. What about your mission was a disappointment to the employees/constituents who have been with you for three years?

   • Nothing lives up to its hype, and about three years into employment or connection is the best time to understand the idealized versus reality picture of mission.

10. Why do your potential donors not give?

    • It is essential to get past the money question to understand what your mission is lacking in the eyes of potential donors.

11. How was your mission reflected in the most difficult decision you made last year?

    • Dissecting the components of a difficult decision lays bare the degree to which mission drives your ministry.

12. Do the unwritten rules of your ministry mirror your mission?

    • Formally we rarely take action that counters the mission, but the unwritten rules of organizational life are the real test of the mission.

13. What organizational policies do you follow that run antithetical to your mission?

    • Laying down every policy against mission may open a new understanding of the positive or negative mission messages you're sending to your stakeholders.

14. How would you summarize your operating budget using mission language rather than money?

- Tying every cost back to the mission, directly or indirectly, reveals the shifts in budgeting or mission focus necessary for optimal operation.

15. Is your mission stronger or weaker than it was three years ago?

- Ministries do not purposefully step away from the mission, but instead, slowly add incongruent ingredients until it is too late to correct the dilution of the mission.

Mission evaluation is an every-day, every-decision, every-relationship task. When you know your mission, you'll know which opportunities fit just right, and which would require changing your lane.

At What Cost?

Having clarity for your mission and a burning passion for fulfilling your calling is central to effective leadership. But alarmingly, some in the church have taken this too far.

We cannot ignore the constant drip of headlines reporting ministry leaders that created a toxic work environment grounded in bullying, belittling, and emotionally abusing those who stand in the way of their mission (which they too often confuse with their ego). Others have cut legal, ethical, and financial corners to achieve their mission, and a few have ignored laws to achieve their objectives.

MISSION FULFILLMENT ALWAYS COMES AT A PRICE—RESOURCES, ENERGY, PEOPLE, AND HEADACHES. BUT YOUR ETHICS, WITNESS, AND STANDARDS OF DECENCY ARE PRICELESS.

No matter how lofty or urgent the mission, where is our witness when the mission ends become more important than the means of achieving them? Yes, there is a risk we won't go as far and as fast in the short run by doing the right thing. But God honors decency in the long run.

When my university first started to offer degrees conveniently designed for working adults, we partnered with a for-profit company specializing in these programs. This company worked with several church-related colleges, including LeTourneau University in Longview, Texas. LeTourneau's branch campus eventually broke free from the company's control and, in doing so, ended that company's presence in Houston, Texas. While my college president friend Bud Austin independently continued his LeTourneau Houston campus, the for-profit school was determined to find another partner to open a branch in that mega-city and asked us to expand into Bud's market.

Moving into a city of that size was a marvelous opportunity for Belhaven, but it would require starting a branch campus within miles of LeTourneau's location. I didn't think that was right—although the company assured me that if we didn't go to Houston, they would establish a branch with one of their other partner institutions.

We had opened branch campuses in Memphis and Orlando. Still, we'd always made it central to our mission only to go where accelerated-format Christian higher education was not being offered. Neither city had a Christ-centered program designed for adult learners when we started.

Opening a Houston campus lined up perfectly with our godly calling, overarching educational mission, and operational strengths. Plus, we knew it would be financially successful too. But I was not comfortable committing to the expansion because another Christian school was already there, and I knew we would siphon students away from them.

Was it right to build our mission reach if it hurt someone else's effectiveness? Would it be right to tout the new venture's lofty goals and hope the means to get there would be left unexamined?

There was only one option. I called Bud and asked if I could come to see him for lunch. We set a time the following week, and I drove five hours each way to talk with him face-to-face.

Having known Bud for years, it didn't take long to lay out the dilemma the for-profit company had created. We could always shoot straight with each other.

Before the waiter even took our order, I put it to him bluntly, "Bud, it would be great for Belhaven if we opened a branch campus in Houston. But—and I absolutely mean this—if it will hurt you, and you'd rather we didn't take their offer, I will tell them no and be just as happy as I would be to tell them yes. I don't want Belhaven to do anything that would hurt you."

Bud has a depth of experience that allowed him to grasp the ramifications of what I was describing. So he didn't answer right away. He was thinking and weighing the issues—he's a very smart president.

I was genuine in my proposal. As much as a branch in Houston would have helped us, would there be any satisfaction in expanding our mission reach, knowing I'd walked all over another Christian university and a president I considered one of my closest peers? Not for me, there wouldn't be. I believed that if Bud asked us not to go, that was God's way of protecting us.

After a long lunch sharing reminiscences, challenges, questions, and vision, plus a little commiserating, we slowly walked to the car. Bud finally answered my question, saying, "Frankly, I'd rather you didn't go to Houston. But that company will come in down the street with another college if you don't go. If I'm going to have enrollment competition, I'd much rather it be you. So go to Houston, and do well. There are enough students to go around."

We opened that campus in Houston and did well for many years—and Bud's campus did too. But, had I not made that long drive for lunch, I know for sure, I never would have enjoyed the subsequent success.

Mission fulfillment always comes at a price—resources, energy, people, and headaches. But your ethics, witness, and standards of decency are priceless.

Mission Control

The International Space Station, an orbiting experimental laboratory, circumnavigates the globe every ninety-two minutes. Although it travels at the speed of just over 17,000 miles per hour, this speed goes mostly unnoticed by those living onboard.

The living conditions and experiments function optimally at an orbit of 240 miles above Earth. But Earth's gravity is constantly pulling the International Space Station off course. Without corrective action by its boosters or a docking rocket, the station would fall to Earth in only 240 days if its path is not regularly tended.

In the same way, our ministry's mission propels us at great speed without us noticing the subtle shifts that pull us off course. If corrected early and often, it is not difficult to keep our mission on track, just as it is with the orbit of the International Space Station. But ignoring mission drift for too long will always lead to catastrophe, just as it would in space travel.

> WHILE MISSION DIRECTION IS THE BOARD AND EVERY EMPLOYEE'S JOB, IT IS FIRST AND FOREMOST THE LEADER'S CHARGE. MISSION CONTROL IS YOUR EVERYDAY RESPONSIBILITY.

Gentle course corrections of your mission must be your highest priority. Without persistent attention, your mission becomes controlled by the gravitational forces of organizational culture, immediate needs, and market forces.

Yes, mission direction is the board's job, as well as every employee's job too. But first and foremost, it is the leader's charge. Mission control is your everyday responsibility.

Chapter 8

Making Decisions That Don't Just Solve the Problem

Ministry leadership requires making a constant stream of decisions. From small issues to significant juncture choices, we can't lead without being decisive. And, don't forget, not making a decision *is* a decision.

The urgent always gets moved to the front of the decision line. In that press, we are tempted to solve the immediate to return our attention to those priorities we consider mission central.

Some decisions are a "T" or "Y" in the road, with apparent alternatives. I've found that most choices are much more subtle shifts, although even the most seemingly insignificant decision is vitally important to those directly impacted. For instance, moving one office into a new space is an important decision for those directly involved, while the change seems insignificant for almost everyone else. But it is not.

Behind most decisions, no matter how small, there is a bearing on the mission. It may not be evident, but it will matter. To stay with this example, to put one workgroup in a better space or more visible space sends an unstated value message about the mission. The same is true of a decision about your vacation policy (valuing restoration for both the employee and the ministry), the flexibility of work hours (valuing needs of families with small children or older employees), and your parking options (valuing hierarchy or not).

A ministry's mission is very rarely purposefully changed, dramatically altered, or abandoned. Instead, the practical demands trigger thousands of decisions that combine their weight to begin a slow and imperceptible drift from the core mission.

Reading this, I'm sure your response is, "That will never happen to us." I pray it won't, but without intention, it will.

It wasn't that many years ago that on Sundays, Christians would never shop, play sports, watch TV, or do much of anything that would distract them from attending two services. They prioritized always being in Sunday School and attending a youth meeting, prayer gathering, or choir practice. Did someone discover a hidden Bible verse that freed up Sunday for what the day has become for most American Christians?

No, but the expansion of convenience stores and electronic check-out make it easy to "quickly run in" to pick up a few essentials, followed later by online shopping. Religious TV took off, and it wasn't hard to change the channel once it was turned on, especially when the NFL moved the Super Bowl to conflict with the time of the Sunday evening service.

The demands of work and the complexity of family pushed Sunday to include more activities that would have been reserved only for a Saturday. Many churches shifted their focus to a single Sunday service and added small group meetings for Sunday evening, eventually drifting to other days to accommodate schedules. And that list goes on into millions of decision permutations for every person, family, community, and local church.

There was never a sole decision to change Sunday priorities. Instead, it was the accumulation of ten thousand small choices that brought about the dramatic shift in how evangelicals now experience Sunday. I'm not judging that one era is better than the other because God and the devil can work with both models. The point is that this slow mission drift was the result of a series of very practical specific decisions. The change was not a purposeful mission adjustment.

In my higher education world, Harvard was founded in 1636 to train pastors under the simple mission: truth. When it was determined that the college's mission drift had become intolerable to theological conservatives, Yale was founded in 1718 to lift up everything Harvard no longer held dear with a more intentional mission: light and truth. No matter their intention, the reality is that both have since moved as far away from their original mission as is possible.

Harvard and then Yale didn't purposefully vacate their evangelical missions. The drift came about in small imperceptible ways as administrators made decisions to solve immediate problems. It was only after they got far enough away from the moorings of their founding mission that they realized it was too late to reconnect.

At decision points, the problem before you is not the only question. The real issue is whether or not you'll tighten your mission grip or relax it. From a hiring choice to your website's look, every decision must be sensitive to the overarching impact on the mission. All decisions tie back to the mission.

FROM A HIRING CHOICE TO YOUR WEBSITE'S LOOK, EVERY DECISION MUST BE SENSITIVE TO THE OVERARCHING IMPACT ON THE MISSION. ALL DECISIONS TIE BACK TO THE MISSION.

The good news is that every problem is an opportunity to reach beyond the immediate issue to strengthen our work's higher calling. You can take advantage of those choices to find a greater purpose in your decision-making.

Solutions Create Problems

Coupled with this care for the mission is the added complexity that decisions envisioned to be solutions instead often plant seeds that grow into even more complex challenges. Understanding this aspect of decision-making is critical because it is in these subsequent choices that ministries fumble the mission question as they attempt to rebound from an initial decision that overlooked its ramifications.

While there are rarely perfect solutions to any problem, only by stepping back from the immediate and framing the challenge in terms of a broader outcome will we see the path to a meaningful solution that is both mission-focused and devoid of downstream problems. Those two issues are always interrelated and co-equal in our decision-making process.

Opportunity Leaders need to develop this dualistic problem-solving outlook purposefully. Traditional planning considers every contingency before taking the first step—although usually missing the moment. But when capturing opportunities, you must build your solutions while in motion. It requires you to make many quick decisions across a rapidly changing landscape.

In your rush, if you become too focused on resolving pressing dilemmas without understanding the potential problems accompanying them, that limited perspective will compound your challenges in this fast-paced model. Subsequently, your solutions will become more cumbersome than the original question. Solution A might solve problem B. But if problem B triggers problems C, D, and E because the fallout wasn't anticipated, you're going backward.

Insightful decision-makers learn to avoid this domino effect. Instead, they link the original solution to the mission while also considering the downstream fallout that could spawn subsidiary problems. Think of it like playing chess. If you're focused only on your next move that allows your rook to escape a pawn, you do not see the challenges that come after the immediate threat. The top chess players in the world report they see fifteen moves ahead. And, since they are considering three or four alternatives to every move, it is no wonder they always win.

One of the essential skills to be developed by Opportunity Leaders is the wisdom to know when to look past the immediate and anticipate several moves ahead on the chessboard. As long as your vision is rooted in the mission, the farther forward you can see, the less likely that your solution to the current problem will become the source of your next challenge.

Policies Are for Cowards

Another way to conceptualize the importance of learning to think about the ramifications of decision-making is to remember that every current policy is a solution to a former problem. Organizations are a collection of policies (written and unwritten) that provide a framework for our values.

Your current policies are a roadmap that can be traced back to very specific problems of your ministry's past:

- two employees start coming to work late—we need an attendance policy
- a few staff members spend too much time shopping online—we need an IT policy
- one person rents a car while others take Uber—we need a travel per diem policy

All the organizational problems of our past are represented in our current policies. And more often than not, those policies were created because of the misconduct of a few outliers to the norm, rather than the whole behaving badly. As a result, most ministry organizations

have become burdened with stifling policies because the earlier decisions were not fully encompassing solutions.

In practice, we tend to create detailed policies to buffer against
the small minority of employees who test, stretch, or take advantage of
the system, as well as those who are simply
angular. We fool ourselves into believing
policies will protect us from needing to
address nonconformists because the very
people we seek to control are the same ones
who are unlikely to change their behavior
unless directly confronted.

**ALL THE
ORGANIZATIONAL
PROBLEMS OF
OUR PAST ARE
REPRESENTED IN
OUR CURRENT
POLICIES.**

Unfortunately, ministries are more
comfortable making a policy for all rather
than confronting the handful of people that
need correction. In my book, *The Longview:
Lasting Strategies for Rising Leaders*, I detailed
shortcomings of leaning on policies as a management tool:

> While employee policies are necessary in every organization,
> Christian organizations oftentimes are most prone to misuse
> them. Why is this? Because biblically centered leaders take
> seriously the command of Jesus in the Sermon on the Mount:
> "Do not judge others, and you will not be judged. . . . Why
> worry about a speck in your friend's eye when you have a log
> in your own? . . . Hypocrite!" (Matt. 7:1–5). Those are seri-
> ous words that should bring us to our knees before carefully
> dealing with any employee difficulty.
>
> Thus, rather than address a sticky personnel issue head-
> on, we tend to gravitate toward creating policies (rules) that
> will "hold us all accountable" without forcing us to specifically
> judge the actions of one over another. To the same degree that
> Christians want to avoid judging individuals, we find comfort

in absolutes to guide us all. But that option is neither theologically sound nor appropriate when it comes to leadership.
We must judge at times, and we can't create one-size-fits-all
absolutes to guide us.[1]

In that book, I challenged leaders to study four questions before
establishing a policy:

1. Does the policy serve your good employees?

2. Are those closest to the problem involved in creating the
   policy?

3. Have you imagined what new problems the policy will create?

4. Will you personally live by the policy?[2]

My conclusion then, as it still is now, is that policies often cause more
problems than they solve. Whenever decisions become a means of
relieving immediate pressure, the solutions probably won't consider
subsequent consequences. Your policy manual will become thicker
and even more burdensome.

But in light of the mission issues raised above and the use of
policies to avoid making decisions, Opportunity Leaders need to
consider an even broader question: Does adhering to a policy limit
the reach of your ministry's mission? If we can't consider an idea
because a policy has already fenced off that area, we may be cut-
ting off opportunities that could become significant if we hadn't first
defaulted to the shield of a policy.

If we'd stuck to our policy at my university, we never would
have launched a creative writing program that would produce one
of America's top-selling authors, Angie Thomas, author of *The Hate
U Give* and other *New York Times* #1 Best Sellers.

Nestled in the heart of Jackson, Mississippi, our university had become a leader in several of the arts, but we didn't work in the field for which our region is best known: writing. William Faulkner, Eudora Welty, John Grisham, and Shelby Foote are known to us through their family connections, not just their prose. So we hired an English faculty member to add a few creative writing courses as electives for English majors to fill the void. But his vision and that of traditional literature study were like mixing oil and water, and it became clear we had ignited a war of cultures and style.

We'd never planned to start a creative writing major, but it was clear we either needed to eliminate the writing courses and lay off the faculty member or break out creative writing into a separate department far away from English. But creating a new academic department just because they couldn't get along broke every rule of our academic policy manual.

In trying to solve the problem with a mission focus rather than being policy directed, the better path was to create a new creative writing department under the School of the Arts, which would have to sink or swim on its own.

A few years later, a quiet, shy African American young woman from a local high school enrolled as a creative writing major. While with us, she wrote a short story that was so captivating, our faculty encouraged her to expand it into a novel. Her book, launched on our campus, *The Hate U Give,* has sold two million copies and received an array of literary awards.

Long before Angie Thomas ever needed Belhaven, a time of philosophical differences among the faculty created an unplanned opportunity for us to begin a creative writing department. Had that not happened, Angie might never have had a Christian environment for developing her art, which God has used enormously to bring the discussion of race, justice, and grace to a new generation.

Innovative solutions are accessible to us when we look past our policies and assure that our decisions are grounded in advancing our mission and not merely solving a pressing problem. As always, no one did this better than Jesus.

Deciding How to Feed 20,000

It is fascinating to examine the only miracle recorded in all four gospels as a textbook example of Jesus addressing a nitty-gritty practical problem and using the occasion to solve a more significant looming problem. He did this while tying all of it back to the mission and tearing up the policy manual.

For over two years, Jesus had been teaching His disciples. He had taught them the truths summarized in the Sermon on the Mount until they could memorize them. He also taught through parables they didn't fully understand at the time because they hadn't grasped the full deity of Jesus. He modeled for them forgiveness, instructed them how to pray, showed them supernatural healing, and introduced them to the kingdom. And they watched and learned, even when overturning social order, chastising the influential and powerful, and prioritizing time for women, children, and those the culture labeled "sinners."

Then, after all this intense training, like college seniors ready for an internship, the Scripture reports He sent them out for several days to work in pairs to multiply their reach. He wanted them to learn ministry on the front lines, not just in supporting what He did. But the assignment was more about what was to come next in the disciples' spiritual growth than who they would encounter in their journey.

When they returned from this bold assignment, I'm sure they were brimming with excitement as they all gathered again, full of stories about casting out demons, healing the sick, preaching, and praying. This was their first time ministering alone in this structured way, and they wanted to tell Jesus and each other all that had happened. To debrief and get restored, Jesus gathered them in their boat to go off alone. That was the plan.

But the news of their ministry spread faster than they could travel, and before reaching shore, people had run ahead to see them. Instead of staying with the plan, Jesus captured an opportunity and began to teach about 5,000 men plus their families. That was probably about 20,000 people in total.

As Jesus was teaching, the disciples had a committee meeting to work on a pressing problem. They were in a remote area, it was getting late, and because no one had planned to be there, they didn't have food. After the discussion, the disciples brought their collective decision to Jesus and asked Him to send the people away into the towns and villages to buy food. This seemed like a reasonable solution to the immediate problem.

Sending the people away to buy food was probably their policy because we have recorded many times Jesus teaching large crowds with no word of how they handled the logistics. To them and us, a policy is always a convenient way to avoid responsibility.

Instead of taking their advice, Jesus said, "You feed them." And with an intense focus on the hunger problem before them, they were bewildered because they argued it would take them months to make enough money to feed that crowd. It wasn't an option. Jesus then asked how much food they did have. A quick inventory turned up a small meal a boy had brought with him of some hard bread and a couple of dried fish.

This unplanned encounter became the framework for one of the most surprising miracles recorded. It is made even more astonishing because Jesus knew that feeding the people wasn't the problem that most needed a solution. Yes, they all were hungry, but Jesus was looking past the pressing problem to what was ahead.

The more critical challenge was how to lift the disciples to a new level of understanding Jesus as the Son of God. Obviously, they didn't understand the full supernatural nature of Jesus because, in their committee meeting, they hadn't even considered a miracle as a way to feed the people (even though they had already seen Jesus perform many other miracles).

Focusing on the mission instead of simply the logistics challenge, Jesus made clear the best option for feeding the people. And we all know the story about twelve baskets of food being left over after He multiplied the five loaves and two fish. Just imagine how the heads of the disciples must have been spinning!

The decision to solve the immediate problem by way of this remarkable miracle was a look fifteen moves down the chessboard when we grasp what happened next. Later that same night, as the disciples were scared to death in a storm, Jesus walked on water to further emphasize His deity. And those back-to-back miracles prepared the way for this transformational exchange recorded in Luke 9:18–20, as Jesus asked His disciples:

> AS LONG AS YOUR VISION IS ROOTED IN THE MISSION, THE FARTHER FORWARD YOU CAN SEE, THE LESS LIKELY THAT YOUR SOLUTION TO THE CURRENT PROBLEM WILL BECOME THE SOURCE OF YOUR NEXT CHALLENGE.

> "Who do people say I am?"
>
> "Well," they replied, "some say John the Baptist, some say Elijah, and others say you are one of the other ancient prophets risen from the dead."
>
> Then he asked them, "But who do you say I am?"
>
> Peter replied, "You are the Messiah sent from God!"

The challenge to feed thousands of famished people was not the problem. Equipping a small band of disciples with the understanding necessary to spread Christianity to the entire world was the larger problem. Jesus solved both in one action.

Decision-making that considers factors beyond immediate

pressure for a solution is a leadership talent requiring dependency on the wisdom of Christ and a commitment to follow a mission-centered pattern of problem-solving.

Decision Dissecting

As we gain experience, we grow in the quality of our decision-making. Each round of our decisions becomes more insightful, long-lasting, multifaceted, and nuanced. But the price of gaining experience can be high, allowing short-sighted or incomplete decisions to become a salve rather than a solution.

Fortunately, there is a way to learn the art of decision-making that anticipates moves down the chessboard, avoids creating new problems, and avoids defaulting to burdensome catch-all policies. When faced with an unwieldy dilemma, rather than immediately diving in to craft a solution for the future, take the time to dissect the history that created the problem. What policies, choices, or structure realignments of the past have joined together to make this your problem now? What lack of collaboration, rush to stomp out an immediate fire, or self-serving perspective crafted the factors that have enabled this issue to reach a breaking point?

Rather than only relying on the bumps and bruises of experience to be your teacher, you can learn to make decisions that will serve you well in the future by pausing and thoughtfully examining the past.

Chapter 9

Getting Out
in Front

My first deep dive into Opportunity Leadership came while I
was still firmly entrenched in executing a traditional planning
model.

I'd just completed a classic comprehensive planning process
with all the appropriate committees, deliberation, and controls in
place. The potential of significant new goals excited my campus as
we all waited in anticipation for the long-range plan's unveiling. The
plan finally produced a stellar document outlining eleven "strategic
agenda" objectives, each with measurable targets under each priority.
It was textbook planning come to life.

We were proud of our plan. It covered the full range of needs,
including academics, spiritual life, athletics, new buildings, finance,
and, of course, parking (every formal plan must address parking). It
was a blueprint we assumed would mark both the direction and the
boundaries of our priorities for many years ahead.

Buried deeply in the plan, positioned where I hoped few would
notice, was the hint of openness to "consider" the addition of football. The idea was bundled in a third-tier action objective with other
potential new sports. Because of my prior experiences, I knew that
a college football team is both a positive and negative force, unlike

anything else in college athletics. If we added it, football would need to be introduced slowly, cautiously, and with a great deal of deliberative planning.

I wanted to keep football in the "maybe–someday" category to not overwhelm those who would be nervous. On the plus side, I knew what it could do to build campus enrollment and morale. But, if not done correctly, it had the potential to become a financial drain and negatively shift the character of the student body. Unfortunately, the disasters were more common for small campuses than the successes, and many schools were eliminating football.

As we finished that plan, I was hopeful that maybe within the next five years, we could consider adding football. That was until God dropped an opportunity in my lap that was too good to pass up.

Starting football was the farthest thing from my mind as I wandered through a group of graduates, parents, and friends following a graduation ceremony in the days just after we had announced our long-range plan. But to my shock, I nearly stumbled over a football coach I had recruited and hired only a few months earlier before leaving the school where I previously served as president.

"What in the world are you doing here in Mississippi?" I nearly shouted at him. Of all the football coaches I'd worked with through the years, this coach was the single best recruiter I'd ever known. More importantly, he had a heart for the gospel and discipleship that was woven into every aspect of leading his team. He knew his X's and O's on the field but understood the higher calling of coaching that went far beyond wins and losses.

"I got fired right after you left," he laughingly responded. I was shocked, and in unpacking the story I learned that he had been diagnosed with cancer, and disappointingly, once his medical condition became public, the school let him go. I was heartbroken for him and shocked they would risk the discrimination claim. Thankfully he was getting treatment, and the prognosis appeared positive. Being the optimistic person he was, he touted being glad to move back closer to home—just a few miles from my new campus.

Standing in front of me was my ideal football coach—unemployed, ready to go, and living down the street. A choice had to be made.

We either reignite the multi-tiered planning process, asking for the grinding gears of evaluation to study the prospect of adding football and its impact on everything else we wanted to do. Or it was time to step way out front alone and become the advocate for starting an intercollegiate football program.

I'd never seen an opportunity moment like this and had to do something out of the ordinary.

"Would you like to start a football team from scratch?" was my blunt question to the coach. A huge smile reached me before his answer, "Would I ever!"

The deal was done. But what had I done? How in the world was I going to explain this to all who had just finished months of work in planning meetings, with little mention of football? We didn't have a stadium, locker room, weight room, training facility, or practice field. We had nothing but the opportunity to hire an ideal coach.

> THE KEY IS TO LEAD THE BAND AS A DRUM MAJOR THAT INSPIRES OTHERS TO FOLLOW, BUT ALSO TO MAKE SURE THE BAND IS STILL WITH YOU. OTHERWISE, YOU'LL LOOK FOOLISH, HIGH-STEPPING ALL ALONE.

More importantly, how could I sell this to the board, much less to skeptical faculty who were still getting to know their new president? What about our other coaches who had identified pressing needs for their teams and would argue their priorities should come before we start any new sports? And then, there were alumni and current students who saw us as a quiet former women's college, not as a brash football school. They were going to go crazy!

It Is Risky Out in Front

Leaders must be willing to get out in front to lead when opportunities are presented. Yes, consensus building, detailed evaluation, and organizational structure will come along as part of testing an idea before implementation. But a leader must take those first vulnerable steps to get out front to champion the idea if advances are to bring about significant change.

Getting out front while holding high the banner of a new opportunity brings risk to your reputation if it fails and criticism for not including others in developing the concept, even if it does work. But the advocacy role also brings great rewards that will move your ministry forward.

Leadership risk is a prerequisite if opportunities are to be captured. Ministries do not take dramatic leaps forward because of their ability to grind data and process materials better than others. Advances often come about because someone is willing to take a God-inspired risk that others are too fearful to tackle.

Out front, you will sometimes be misinterpreted for being pushy, autocratic, reckless, or independent. All those criticisms are valid if you get TOO FAR out front. The key is to lead the band as a drum major that inspires others to follow, but also to make sure the band is still with you. Otherwise, you'll look foolish, high-stepping all alone.

Before moving out front, double-check your motives with a spiritual barometer to ensure your push is never self-serving. Here are a few ways you can do this:

- Ask a respected advisor or two if what you're considering is self-serving or best for the ministry. If you invite transparency, they will tell you the truth.

- Put it before the Lord and ask for clarity to assure your motives are pure. This is like a prayer for patience—don't pray it if you don't want to be tested.

- Imagine the best that could happen for you personally if what you're considering went forward, and what is the worst that could happen. If the scale is tilted too far either direction, it is time to pause and question your intentions.

After you've checked your motives, as a leader you will discover three common risks when you get out front.

1. Risk in Not Knowing

In capturing a new opportunity, the only thing you'll know for sure is how much you don't know. Those who wait to collect all the data and analyze all the angles don't provide leadership; they merely oversee bureaucracy. In contrast, Opportunity Leaders will know little when they take those first steps but are willing to walk in the light they have at the time.

There will be tons of unanswered questions tangled up with every opportunity. But gathering accurate answers to your questions is not the biggest obstacle ahead. The immense challenge is not knowing what you don't even yet know to ask. This double layer of ambiguity puts most ministries into a bind that keeps them immobile until long after the opportunity has passed.

When you're out in front, this lack of answers will make you feel vulnerable. But wise leaders have learned to minimize that exposure by having immersed themselves in an understanding of their ministry's mission and culture, even if they can't anticipate answers to the challenges of a specific opportunity.

In starting football, I took the idea directly to the source of where resistance would build. Our campus had a proud tradition of success in soccer, winning a national championship in prior years. So my first stop to advocate for football was not with the board chair, but with the soccer coach. It took a very long time to bring the soccer loyalists around, but at least I knew where my challenge was because I understood the culture.

> IN CAPTURING A NEW OPPORTUNITY, THE ONLY THING YOU'LL KNOW FOR SURE IS HOW MUCH YOU DON'T KNOW. THOSE WHO WAIT TO COLLECT ALL THE DATA AND ANALYZE ALL THE ANGLES DON'T PROVIDE LEADERSHIP; THEY MERELY OVERSEE BUREAUCRACY.

You'll need to know your mission and culture from top to bottom. Not just how it is expressed in mission statements and policies, but how it is lived out through your stakeholders. When you understand your ministry through their eyes, then you'll be able to more accurately anticipate which new opportunities are likely to fit and which would be incongruent with your values and gifts. The more you invest in this understanding, the likelihood of your success will rise, and your vulnerability will become minimized.

2. Risk in Improvising

With every new opportunity, you'll need to learn to get started and then fix it later. This pattern is not theoretical in Opportunity Leadership but standard practice. You'll never have all the information, people, resources, or tools you'll need to "get started right."

Improvising is foundational to successfully capturing opportunities. You'll need to shift, adjust, and adapt to changing circumstances at many points in the journey. Go into this knowing some stakeholders will become extremely uncomfortable with your improvisation. They won't want to go forward unless you can give assurances and concrete answers to every key question. At that point, you'll have to determine the value of pushing ahead, even if questioning and grumbling intensifies.

Every situation is different, and only you can decide how hard to push or if you should back off. But in every circumstance, it is predictable that if you get backed into a corner promising absolutes, one of two things will happen:

1. You'll never capture opportunities because being sure of the path forward is not possible when God brings new opportunities. After all, if you can see the path to the finish line, you do not need to trust the Lord. Why would God give a golden opportunity to those unwilling to trust Him for the unknown? Making hard promises limits your options for even beginning, much less making adjustments as a new opportunity matures.

2. You will have to make lots of changes after you get started. The outcome probably won't look like what's envisioned at the beginning. You'll learn new things, incorporate new people, and find twists and turns you never expected. But if you make unqualified promises about A, B, and C before you start, then your constituency will not trust you even if some alternative outcome of X, Y, and Z is highly successful. A spirit of pliability up front is your only option.

Opportunity Leadership is not for the faint of heart. It requires the courage to improvise. Like Abraham, it takes resolution to trust God without knowing the destination. Like Peter, it takes valor to do it God's way when you think you know better. Like Uzziah, it takes nerve to rely on God alone. Improvisation that is God-directed creates a dynamic of leadership that is inspirational. When God brings an opportunity, it is not a single jolting turn, and then we are left to fend on our own. For Christian leaders, improvising is not "winging it" because we have the assurance that the Lord is the one truly leading.

As in my football experience, the unexpected encounter with the coach was only the first of an astonishing series of opportunities that were beyond anything we ever could have planned. The series of remarkable people and moments that came afterward was like watching the hand of God going before us to open every door.

Most notably, the ideal football coach around which we built the entire project took a turn for the worst medically. At that point, we were too far into it to turn back, but he was to be the lynchpin in the entire project, and now we had to improvise.

A long story, made somewhat shorter, is that Norman Joseph was a highly acclaimed college quarterback at Mississippi State and then went on through the coaching ranks to become offensive coordinator at the University of Southern Mississippi, of Brett Favre fame. Norman had become an extremely successful assistant coach, but when word leaked that he had interviewed at another school, his head coach fired him. That is football.

Although my ideal coach was no longer available, God knew that Norman was just who we needed to start the program and lead our new team. He was already well known to every high school coach in our state and the sports media. Norman is the only coach in NAIA history to produce both a 1,000-yard rusher and 1,000-yard receiver in a program's first two seasons in existence while leading us to a top twenty-five national ranking in only our second year.

IT IS THROUGH SHIFTS AND ADJUSTMENTS THAT YOU'LL DEEPEN YOUR DEPENDENCY ON GOD FOR THE PATH AHEAD AND HAVE A FRONT-ROW SEAT TO WATCH HIM WORK.

While improvising exposes a leader to criticism, it is the only way to move significant opportunities forward. But more importantly, it is through these shifts and adjustments that you'll deepen your dependency on God for the path ahead and have a front-row seat to watch Him work.

3. Risk in Reviving

Think of every opportunity as its own "business start-up" that follows a well-known pattern: (1) launch, (2) existence, (3) survival, (4) traction, and then (5) stability. But your challenges are not in the rearview mirror if you reach this point where most declare success.

The lessening of start-up intensity will usher in an increased pattern of confidence as the new venture becomes established. This "reviving" phase will be as critical as the launch if long-term success is achieved. Predictably, this (6) contentment stage will be followed by a period of (7) chaos and confusion that will trigger (8) choices and change.

Out in front, leadership is not reserved for launching, but this critical phase of reviving will also demand your strength and visibility. Responding to the complexity of this readjustment stage will be even more demanding than the initial start-up. If you don't speak up when turmoil infiltrates, no one else will, and the dream will spiral downward.

We hit this mark about eight years into what we considered had become a well-established football program. Our hopes were high, but that fall, the team got off to a horrible start. In response, I did something I've never done as a college president—I asked our second-year coach if I could talk to his team about their season.[1]

In the middle of the week after that sixth loss, I was speaking for a luncheon event. Our coach was in the audience to be supportive. However, I could see his mind was elsewhere. The coach had been through a tough personal challenge with a gravely ill wife who required life-threatening surgery and a brand new baby at home. So when I saw him that day, he looked like he just needed someone to lean on, and he jumped at the opportunity for me to speak to the team.

Through the years, I've become used to making a speech at a moment's notice about almost any topic. But I had no idea what I was going to say as I walked onto the practice field that afternoon. And when you're standing in the middle of one hundred sweaty big football players in full pads, it is an intimidating place to be crafting an outline. I just prayed for God to give a word that might help.

As I looked into their eyes, all of a sudden, I didn't see football players in helmets, but young men who will become husbands and fathers, men who will be employees and employers, football players who will soon be community and church members. At that moment, God prompted me to say something like this:

> Guys, this season is no longer about football, but it is about the rest of your lives. What you do with the second half of this season will set your course. You can place blame, you can get mad, you can call it unfair, you can give up, and you can make excuses.
>
> Or you can pull together, look ahead with hope, and do well what you're trained to do. It is time to dig down deep, make a fresh start to overcome the tough circumstances, and commit your future to the Lord. Because how you respond to this football season will determine how you deal with adversity for the rest of your life.

And I went on to suggest they consider this a brand new season, starting with the coming Saturday, and begin with a 0–0 record for the year (even though six losses were already in the books).

Now, after a speech like that, you'd think they would have lifted me on their shoulders and marched to the administration building in triumph or thrown me in the lake. But instead, there was no reaction. Zero.

I don't know what the coach did after that, but we won by three points on Saturday. The following week, we ran up the score with a comfortable win. And, the third week, this reenergized team defeated a team who had gotten the best of us too many times.

By the start of the fourth week, they were a team on fire. But when you're down by four points with only twenty seconds left and sixty-two yards between you and the end-zone, you've got to believe God smiled on us for three games, and that's good enough. Astonishingly, our desperation pass bounced off a defender's helmet and into the arms of our fastest receiver, who had a clear path to a touchdown.

By the time we kicked off the fifth game, this team had gone from the lowest lows to the highest of the highs. And then, they found themselves low again as they were down by fifteen points going into the fourth quarter. The following twenty unanswered points we scored were more than just good play calling for this refocused team. Finally, we topped the season off with a homecoming win, passing out to the team the "undefeated second season" shirts we had preordered.

My God-inspired challenge to the team may or may not have won us football games, but from what the players and coaches reported, God helped all to see the more significant objectives of this floundering football program. I could not have intervened at all, but I knew the trajectory was headed for disaster.

Getting out front again was a huge risk, both for me personally and for the institution. They could have lost the remaining six games, just like they did the first six. Or they might have won a few games, but nothing would have changed at the core of the football program.

Instead, the football program passed through the chaos and confusion stage that is part of every new opportunity. Today, our football team plays on campus in one of the most beautiful small college stadiums in America (shared with soccer) and lead by a coach of enormous strength and vision. Wins and losses on the field will always go up and down, but our football team is victorious in measuring what matters most as a Christian institution.

Chapter 10

Practicing Future-Focused Evaluation

D uring his eighteen-month meteoric rise from an itinerant firewood peddler to Civil War commander, Ulysses S. Grant demonstrated the aggressiveness that President Abraham Lincoln had been begging to see from his troops. Domineering in the bloodiest days of the war during the battles of Belmont, Fort Henry, Fort Donelson, and Shiloh, Grant convinced the president he was willing to fight.

As the army moved on toward Vicksburg to cut off the South's primary supply route, Grant was also responsible for controlling the illegal cotton trade that was refueling the South's crippled economy. Closing a porous border between two warring parties that had always traded freely was a nearly impossible assignment.

On December 17, 1862, stepping out on authority he may not have had, Grant made a decision that would have gotten him fired by almost any boss—that is, except Abraham Lincoln.

Issuing General Order No. 11, Grant expelled "Jews as a class" from the region under his command—Tennessee, Mississippi, and Kentucky—believing that illegal cotton was being smuggled to the North "mostly by Jews and other unprincipled traders."[1] At the time, Grant was headquartered in Holly Springs, Mississippi, in what is now the president's home at Rust College. And, on that same day in

Holly Springs, Grant had Jewish families rounded up and forced to immediately leave on foot with only what they could carry.

Understandably, Grant was under tremendous stress because of mounting frustration from the entangled Vicksburg campaign, the impending expiration of soldiers' deployment terms, and the continual rearmament of the South directly tied to the proceeds from illegal cotton sales. Buffering these tensions, Grant was emboldened by his string of battlefield successes grounded in aggressiveness that elevated his leadership stature and reputation. The juxtaposition of his outlook, coupled with his inexperience in command, triggered Grant to naively issue the prejudicial order, even over his advisors' objections.

Like all leaders throughout history who have made poor decisions unable to stand up to scrutiny, Grant's judgment was not grounded in facts alone but emotion. General Order No. 11 was issued shortly after a contentious visit from his father, Jessie Root Grant, who had traveled to Mississippi from Illinois. His father came to visit his son with two Jewish merchants seeking special treatment in the sale of cotton. This bold and illegal request further incited Grant's long-contentious relationship with his domineering father. Whether intended or not, Grant's action against the Jews was a tangible way to push back at his father's control.

General Order No. 11 generated outcry from the public across both the South and the North, as well as a rebuke from Democrats in Congress who quickly brought to the floor a bill to censure Grant. Most importantly, the president did not defend him. Lincoln privately told Grant that he was wrong, and publicly supported the Jews and denounced his military commander.

Just seventeen days after the order was first issued on January 3, 1863, the president himself rescinded the directive ostracizing Jews. In private correspondence, Lincoln made clear to Grant that the decision was a harsh and miscalculated judgment. Further, it had consequences far beyond the immediate problem Grant was attempting to solve.

Lincoln was literally in the process of drafting the Emancipation Proclamation when Grant muddied the waters with General Order No. 11.

The remarkable element in this saga is that less than a month after Grant was bluntly corrected by the commander-in-chief, President Lincoln promoted Grant, giving him overall command of the Vicksburg campaign.

Bolstered by the president's vote of confidence so quickly following his public failure, Grant's battlefield successes multiplied. His rapid rebound from failure lead Grant to eventually be named the highest-ranking commander of Union forces. With his defeat of Lee at Appomattox, Grant made a bold decision to offer shockingly generous surrender terms focused on the future rebuilding of the South, rather than blaming them for seceding from the Union.

The new national hero adapted his mentor's approach to future-focused evaluation. Later, Grant used it well during two terms in the White House as president, leading progressive reconstruction and racial equality initiatives across the Southern states he had conquered.

Future-Focused Evaluation

This future-focused rebuke of Lincoln toward Grant is reminiscent of the words of Jesus to the woman caught in adultery: "Go and sin no more" (John 8:11). Jesus didn't chronicle her mistakes, add to her weight of guilt, or require a subscription to specific accountability guidelines. He simply set her on a better course for the future rather than prosecuting the past.

In both Jesus' and Lincoln's case, the leader was attacked for the costly mistake of someone else. For Jesus, the Pharisees attempting to trick Him into heresy was the equivalent of the opposition in Lincoln's Congress. And both had enormous crowds of critics studying how they handled the errors they were forced to arbitrate.

We need to learn from these models when the people we work with make costly blunders. If you're in leadership for very long at all, you'll find yourself in the same position as Lincoln and Jesus, over and over again.

Running counter to most leaders' typical evaluation outlook, Jesus and Lincoln were future-focused rather than backward-correcting in addressing the missteps of someone under their care. This is a talent that Opportunity Leaders must develop to avoid quashing the entrepreneurial spirit of a ministry.

When a serious mistake is made, organizational evaluation tends to focus far too much on seeking to assign blame. We parse out the assumed motives, extenuating circumstances, lack of training, lax supervision standards, and character flaws of the offender, hoping to pinpoint why anyone could make such a mistake. But, more often than not, bad decisions are usually rooted in inexperience, limited perspective, fear of mistakes, intense pressure, and/or a host of issues completely unrelated to the workplace. Although too often the blinders of selfishness or merely poor judgment cause the error, it is rarely nefarious intentions that drive bad decisions.

Old-school accountability approaches believe forward growth is impossible unless the root problem is identified and eradicated. Based on that assumption, backward-correcting rather than forward-focused leaders identify what they consider to be the origin of the deficiency and set a corrective course that seeks to

1. restrict authority so that the error in question does not become a pattern;

2. accentuate power differentials so that offenders better understand their place in the hierarchy;

3. heap on about as much guilt as possible, assuming that a load of guilt will slow down further erroneous action.

Does this sound familiar? Of course, it does! You've probably been corrected just like this when you were at a lower rung on the leadership ladder. And just like bad teachers who subsequently lead their own classroom in the same way their bad teachers taught them, leaders replicate the evaluation approach of their personal experience—even when they know it was not effective.

Compounding the feebleness of this misguided assessment pattern, we add simplified grading scales to formal reviews, gossipy 360 evaluations, and link reviews with raises. These are tools that only elevate tension instead of cultivating growth. At their core, these misguided employee evaluation systems are built around elevating the power of the evaluator rather than addressing the needs of the one being evaluated.

I strongly believe in evaluation, but how we do it too often crushes the spirit of the people we lead. I've discussed the purpose of accountability and offered detailed alternative evaluation techniques in a chapter of my previous book, *The Longview*, entitled "The Bookends of a Leader's Character—Evaluation and Accountability." Summarizing the importance of this critical component of leadership, I conclude:

> The long-term consequences of a life without correction and accountability are staggering. Neglecting effective evaluation may momentarily feel like escaping a checkup with the dentist, but over time, a mouthful of root-canal work will be much more painful than the preventive visit. Accountability to a board, boss, spouse, coworkers, and even your children is God's gift to each of us to assure we strive for lasting quality in our lives. . . .
>
> Without these two bookends to hold us upright we are destined for a life of tragedy, failure, and mediocrity—which may come later than sooner, but it will come.[2]

The question is not if we evaluate—we must. But contrary to the norm, I'm recommending evaluations focused on strengthening rather than controlling, teaching rather than correcting, and looking forward rather than placing blame.

Before leaving the topic of deficiencies embedded in typical evaluation practices, I must address one more evaluation myth that runs rampant in leadership, specifically in the church.

Imprudently, many leaders believe it is their Shakespearian duty to make this promise to those in their charge, "No matter how bad your mistakes, I'll unwaveringly stand with you in public, and will only correct you in private." That is the right way to handle these situations when the blunder impacts procedures and processes, but when it comes to mission or conflicts that hurt others, that approach is 100 percent wrong.

When an employee's mistake strikes at the core of your mission or threatens others, leaders must speak out to publicly defend the ministry's higher calling. Jesus did this with the woman caught in adultery, and Lincoln did with Grant. Both expressly disavowed their decision while keeping their protégé future-focused.

Grace-Filled Accountability

As leaders, we may feel a scolding is well deserved for an employee's erroneous action, but that usually only compounds the difficulty. Opportunity Leadership creates a culture of thorough and transparent analysis—including self-evaluation—that concentrates on problems, not people.

Too many leaders repeatedly solve the same problem because they cannot reflect on what went wrong without triggering a desire to place blame. Instead of pointing fingers of blame, if we could transparently evaluate mistakes, complexities, and partial successes, our insights would guide us to new solutions with lasting success.

Yes, sometimes the most gracious thing you can do for someone is to hold them very specifically accountable. Teaching others to meet deadlines, aim for higher-level work, and produce under pressure may not feel like generosity to them at the time, but you are graciously teaching important work patterns before the stakes get higher.

In those moments when accountability correction must be articulated, extend grace by focusing those you lead on the bigger goals you're helping them achieve. The purpose of accountability, judgment, and evaluation must always be the growth of those God has entrusted you to guide. It's never to belittle, control, or scorn them. One way to think about it is: accountability serves as the guardrails, but grace is the road.

To develop a future-focused evaluation approach, I would suggest seven handles designed to strengthen your ministry team rather than place blame.

1. One Size Does Not Fit All

We want evaluation to be fair to everyone—that is how we must be. But fair doesn't mean the standard or the process is the same for all employees.

As a parent, would you set identical house rules for all three of your children, ages five, twelve, and seventeen? And when they break those rules, would you correct each of them in the same way? Of course not. Why do we expect every employee to be at the same level of giftedness, experience, insight, and temperament? Our evaluation standards, methods, and styles should be equally varied.

If you focus on helping people grow from where they are instead of being "fair" by judging them all by the same standard and with the same tools, you'll begin to see your team flourish. If not, the capable people who easily clear the bar will slack off, and the weak employees will live under a cloud of intimidation.

2. Teach Something New

If I could be granted one wish across all organizational cultures, it would be to substitute the word "teacher" for "supervisor"—or for Christian ministries, it should be "discipler." Whether it be a formal annual review or a stand-up consultation, every evaluation moment should be value-added to the person whose life and success we're responsible for enriching. Be a teacher, not an overseer.

The workplace should be a purposeful learning environment. Apple, Google, Disney, and other innovative companies figured this out first, and all their employees are tasked with continuous learning as they grow in responsibility. Being able to stretch, stumble, and question—and then do it all over again—are at the heart of the learning cycle.

> WHETHER IT BE A FORMAL ANNUAL REVIEW OR A STAND-UP CONSULTATION, EVERY EVALUATION MOMENT SHOULD BE VALUE-ADDED TO THE PERSON WHOSE LIFE AND SUCCESS WE'RE RESPONSIBLE FOR ENRICHING.

Don't lose sight of the hard reality that some people need more laps around the track than others in learning to achieve successful outcomes. Give people room to make mistakes, experiment, test solutions, and fail at times. When you do, they learn. And, if they cannot learn how to grow in their job, then you've got a different problem that goes back to either (1) not hiring right, or (2) placing someone in the wrong position at the wrong time. But I'll talk more about this issue in the next chapter.

3. Coach for Insight

There is a difference between placing blame and helping someone examine what caused their mistakes. If you can do the second in a non-threatening way, you can help them grow beyond what they ever imagined and become of greater usefulness in ministry.

I had a new unit leader who became so distraught with his team during a group meeting that he used some strong and inappropriate words to try to shock them into attentiveness. That, we had to address. But in digging down, we discovered his previous bosses in the business world were verbally threatening when a group was unresponsive, and he transposed their poor behavior into his new ministry setting.

Of course, in a secular business setting, that language was hardly noticed because off-color adjectives are common. But in our environment, it was not just an expletive bomb, but an atomic bomb—prompting one on his team to resign. Once he understood that his background was limiting his future, he quickly made the adjustments and grew in the job.

With a little assuring coaching, I've found that people who make mistakes can usually figure out where they went wrong and put in place their own corrective course.

4. Don't Hint

It seems like on every New Year's Day that I make the same resolution: I'm not going to hint to those I work with, and instead, bluntly articulate my expectations. And every year, I slide back into a pattern of hinting.

I work regularly with an extremely strong, gifted, experienced, and capable team. In tracking their "mistakes" that frustrate me, I can nearly always follow the problem back to me hinting rather than being direct. Appropriately, I try to resist "telling them what to do," but it's not fair to expect them to read my mind either—even after working closely with me for many years. Too often, my desire to be telepathic is where we run into trouble. That's on me.

In my effort to stop this pattern of hinting at my wishes and instead be more direct in giving direction, I've found two priorities to be helpful:

1. Detail your expectations in writing.

2. Build assignments around each person's gifting rather than always trying to work around their weaknesses.

If leaders become more direct, occasional conversations might be more often pointed, but crisis confrontations can probably be avoided altogether as small corrections steer the course.

5. Provide a New Challenge

Unless employees don't care or are lazy, they all believe they are using their time wisely and making correct decisions. So in most cases, when people mess up and see their errors, they want to show you they can do it right the next time.

Our challenge as leaders is to realize that when someone fails, they will not hear our criticism as addressing only the task, even though we intend that boundary. A negative evaluation strikes at the core of their judgment, effort, skills, and character. Performance evaluations are not just about work; they are taken as a personal attack.

Break free from the traditional model of deflating correction. If you provide forward-focused guidance, employees will be anxiously looking for a new opportunity to demonstrate their capabilities and regain your trust.

Unfortunately, leaders tend to curtail opportunities for those who disappoint rather than offer new challenges that provide a platform to demonstrate the wisdom gleaned from previous failures. When possible, if you can give a new and stretching assignment to the one you've corrected, it provides an opportunity to exercise the new skills they have learned.

Even more importantly, pushing them forward demonstrates your confidence in them. Nothing will accelerate their restoration more than being entrusted with a fresh challenge.

6. Build Accountability Safeguards for All

Before there is a problem, create safeguards that remove the temptation or pressure to make errant choices. You will protect everyone by preemptively closing off predictably troublesome paths.

For example, you are doing a great favor for your employees and yourself when you build in strict systems eliminating the opportunity to use a ministry credit card or petty cash improperly. Even in Christian ministries, people are regularly fired for stealing.

Creating systems that make abuse difficult is not being hard on employees; it is being kind to them. Establishing strong accountability safeguards will cut off the temptation before it becomes a problem that could destroy their career.

Whether the issue is money, character, time, relationships, or ego, more accountability and transparency are nearly always better than less. People who do not have accountability built into their life systems will almost always run off the rails. It is heartbreaking when I've had to confront mature and experienced Christians who I could never have anticipated would crash and burn, simply because they didn't have accountability in one aspect of their life.

Having to fire someone for inappropriate behavior is always distressing for a ministry, and, of course, dismissal is life-crushing for the one who went outside the lines. One person's sins often damage the overall ministry as funds, credibility, and influence shrink, and sadly, the pain trickles down on those who have served faithfully.

It is always more effective for the devil to attack from inside than outside. He's after your team—and you.

7. If You Don't Accept Criticism, Why Should They?

If you don't learn, grow, and change when confronted with criticism, why should those who work with you be responsive to your correction?

The historical path of big personality Christian leaders failing is always similar. They insulate themselves from accountability and dismiss criticism as attacks from fools. But I have found there is usually something helpful to be learned from every criticism—even an unreasonable, unfair, and unfounded attack.

Be less defensive of criticism. I guarantee you won't like it because nobody likes to be criticized, but it will make you a more effective leader.

They Will Grow

Ulysses Grant "got it" when Lincoln evaluated him by focusing on the future instead of the past. For the rest of his life, Grant looked for ways to make up for issuing General Order No. 11.

He was the first American president to ever raise human rights for Jewish people as a foreign policy issue, attend a synagogue, or appoint a cadre of Jews to important government posts, including Edward Salmon as Territorial Governor of Washington.

Near the end of Grant's two terms as president, Rabbi Isaac Mayer Wise—who had aggressively campaigned against Grant in the first presidential election—said, "President Grant has revoked General Grant's notorious order No. 11."[3] Rabbi Wise recognized the dramatic effort of Grant to correct his past.

We don't know what happened to the woman caught in adultery. We know a mob nearly stoned her, and then the Savior of the world protected her life and let her move on without a scolding. After that, I can't imagine that her life wasn't transformed when the cacophony demanding her death was quieted. And, in its place, a single calm voice guided her to simply "go and sin no more."

Let go of your old evaluation patterns, and try the forward-focused way Jesus taught us; that's what Lincoln did.

Chapter 11

Emulating Baseball Managers Instead of Football Coaches

College football coaches have become today's benchmark of organizational leadership excellence. Gridiron leaders are admired for their firm grip of control on every aspect of their program and their extremely low tolerance for anything short of excellence.

The best ones direct every action on the field, along with controlling their players' diets, academics, relationships, and minute-by-minute daily schedules. No detail is too small, as they run the management of their locker room with the same precision as their game plans. There is nothing that happens within their organization that the winningest coaches do not orchestrate.

Our societal values have elevated football coaches to the pinnacle of admired leadership, with the highest-paid government employee in twenty-nine of fifty states being a university football coach. In the most recent playoffs, the top four college coaches earned $27 million, while in contrast, all fifty United States governors' collective salary was only $7 million. Money speaks to what we admire.

Especially in Christian circles, at every level of the game from high school through the NFL, football coaches have become the church's superstars. For a good reason, this appreciation is well deserved, as they use their influential public platform to proclaim a Christian witness.

The Wrong Model for A Different Game

Leaders committed to traditional planning idealize football coaches as role models because of their commitment to meticulous preparation, the anticipation of every contingency, pinpoint execution, and an intolerance for mistakes. These coaches' leadership formula is essential for winning football games; other models don't work for this intense sport. But these sideline titans are not the right models for organizational leaders seeking to be flexible enough to capture opportunities rather than being limited to the confines of traditional planning.

Instead, as a model for opportunity-focused leaders, consider the role of a baseball manager who encourages players to improvise without supervision, has few plays to call, and cannot make substitutions without eliminating a player from the game entirely. Most importantly, a baseball manager understands that the players assigned to each of the nine positions on the diamond are uniquely gifted and prepared. The manager supports and guides each athlete differently because every baseball player sees and plays a very different game, depending on their designated point of responsibility.

As in any sport, the speed, size, quickness, strength, and skill vary among players for each position on a team. But in football, players often change positions. Offensive linemen can shift among the five blocking positions, a running back could easily play tight end, and many quarterbacks tend to run as much as they throw. And, of course, in soccer, basketball, hockey, softball, lacrosse, and volleyball, players tend to roam with great latitude.

Contrary to most sports, in baseball, each player's idiosyncratic responsibilities are especially distinctive. The quickness of a shortstop would be squandered if he was to play catcher. The graceful long reach of a first baseman would look lumbering and uncoordinated should he play third base. The pure power of a relief pitcher, who throws a ball sixty feet from a stationary platform at ninety-five miles per hour, would be a failure as a right fielder required to make throws twice that length while on the run.

Like successful opportunity-focused ministry leaders, winning baseball managers seek to match every player's attributes, temperament, training, and gifting with each position's uniqueness on the team. The manager further understands that the preparation, intensity, exertion, and rhythm of a pitcher's game are entirely different from a center fielder or shortstop and gives latitude for these individual distinctives. Plus, a manager is always considering how to best use the cadre of players in the dugout and bullpen, waiting to be called into service with only a moment's notice of preparation.

Unlike football, even how each baseball player sees the field of play is dramatically different depending on their position. A catcher is the only player able to see the entire field with a panoramic view while simultaneously keeping an eye out for any hint of a flaw in the batter standing inches over him. In contrast, without the help of a jumbotron, an outfielder can't even see the face of the batter one hundred yards away and won't know the trajectory of a hit ball until an instant before it becomes his responsibility.

Getting the right player in the right position at the right time is a momentous decision for a baseball manager. When the Hall of Famer Cal Ripken Jr. was shifted from shortstop to third base, less than forty feet away from his long-time playing position, it was considered a risky transition, even though he was an elite player. In baseball and ministry organizations, moving someone just slightly out of or adjusting them slightly into their sweet spot will completely alter their effectiveness. Those decisions call for the leader to be both perceptive and courageous.

Baseball managers understand all players are not equal in their strategic importance, and identify the lynchpin people on their team who make the difference between winning or losing. The first four players in the batting lineup are not placed in that order by accident. Likewise, the rotation of starting pitchers is a critical choice.

> RELAX YOUR CONTROL, AND ENCOURAGE YOUR PEOPLE TO BE INDIVIDUALS. IN DOING SO, THEY WILL BECOME STRONGER TEAMS.

The leader develops multiple strategies to take advantage of each player's unique strengths while simultaneously analyzing how they compensate for others' weaknesses. Plus, an effective big league manager helps guide every player to develop their talents and gifts, working with players at every level of the organization, from high school draftees through the mega-millionaire superstars.

At the same time, baseball managers are not the elected head of a democracy tethered to groupthink. A baseball manager is responsible for setting direction, making tough decisions, balancing resources, and bearing the weight of failure. Just like a football coach, there is no doubt they are in charge of their ball club in full.

Like organizations reliant on traditional planning versus those seeking opportunities, football and baseball are two very different games. Football is a metaphor for the game of "efficient implementation" that ministries have played well for decades; baseball is the game of "creative resourcefulness" that our organizations must play for the future.

- Football values power; baseball rewards anticipation.

- Football is plotting; baseball is reactionary.

- Football demands precise coordination; baseball requires personal ingenuity.

- Football is time-pressured; baseball is flowing.
- Football stresses control; baseball demands flexibility.
- Football is relentless; baseball is irregular.
- Football follows a predetermined path to achieve a singular goal; baseball encourages the agility to capture multiple opportunities that achieve interwoven purposes.
- Football requires winning nearly every game to be successful at the highest level; a top baseball team will lose 30 percent of their games.

The divergent objectives of football and baseball call for different leadership skills, outlooks, and even styles. (I'm sure those in the coaching profession identify much deeper levels of intricacy, but those of us who are fans only have access to their public persona.)

Most football coaches constantly prowl the sidelines, talking primarily into a headset to those "upstairs" while barking orders at players because a forty-second play-clock hurries decisions. These leaders must exude confidence and courage, with a "large-and-in-charge" presence, to players who are anxious to prove their worth to the coach.

Baseball managers tend to be settled into a stationary dugout viewing point, often appearing distracted in conversation with various players and coaches. As a game without time limits, they have the luxury of learning from each player's experience as the game progresses, conferring with advisors at all levels and nuancing decisions.

Rather than simply addressing the current challenge, they reflectively strategize multidimensional solutions, continually anticipating challenges that will likely arise later in the game or even future games. Most importantly, to effectively manage the long haul of shifting circumstances, they always keep as many options open as possible.

Change Your Game

Discernable insights gained by examining the revealed differences between these two athletic camps may be enough to get you started developing new leadership talents. Specifically, I'd recommend cultivating three "game-changing" priorities to equip you as an Opportunity Leader to emulate baseball managers instead of football coaches.

1. Encourage Independence

Leaders have spent the last generation extolling the virtues of team cohesion as a primary tool of administration. In a planning model built on decisions from above, work teams able to execute at a football squad's synchronization level are critical for effectiveness. But this model is of the past.

To implement the fresh approach of Opportunity Leadership, we must break through the assumption that building team unity is management's gold standard. A cottage industry of consultants, authors, and keynote speakers has advocated stronger teams as the antidote to nearly every organizational challenge. Even though this focus has generated increasing billable hours for the experts, organizational success has not accrued at the same rate.

Just like leaders fear abandoning their investment in traditional planning without a viable alternative, team building has become engrained as the default leadership tool because a meaningful substitute has not been offered. Even though we know this focus is a severely inadequate solution for most challenges, we dutifully stick with it.

Instead, like a baseball manager, ministry leaders need to empower every employee to envision, explore, experiment, and exercise their ingenuity as they approach their task. Using their distinct perspective, gifting, and style, we will be shocked at the ownership and creativity they will bring to their responsibility if we encourage their independence.

My father, a long-term college president, always described faculty members as "someone who thinks otherwise." People of such high-level expertise see the world differently, which is why I enjoy them. David Hubbard, the long-time president of Fuller Seminary in my dad's past era, characterized faculty as "angular people." Doesn't nearly everyone in a ministry organization now fit these descriptions? A generational shift in organizational culture from uniformity to personal expression has altered how we work together. IBM required all their executives to wear grey suits and white shirts with dark ties until Steve Jobs and his Apple colleagues came to their meetings in tee shirts and jeans. Times have dramatically changed as we've moved from uniformly aligned desks to telecommuting in only one generation.

A dramatic shift in people's workplace expectations is why continuing to press for team cohesion will generate increasingly diminishing returns. For too long, organizational leaders have prized team harmony over ingenuity. If we take off the constraints and start to enjoy the "angles" and "otherwise thinking" of our employees, we'll gain advantages that flow from people released to use all their God-given gifts.

Will your teams still have conflicts you'll have to arbitrate? Of course! Did your years of focusing on team cohesion keep you from having personal tensions between team members? Of course not!

Especially as we invite younger generations into our ministry organizations, typical team building controls will chafe at their instincts, and we'll either run them off or dramatically dilute their gifts. These generations are passionate about your mission, not about the rules for how you work together.

Relax your control, and encourage your people to be individuals. In doing so, they will become stronger teams.

2. Reverse the Spotlight

Leaders are so accustomed to receiving affirmation and recognition that they assume such praise is a normal part of everyone's life. It is not.

After the Sunday morning service, a pastor stands at the exit to greet churchgoers and is showered with words of appreciation for even a mediocre message. A ministry CEO is introduced to a small group of visitors, and they applaud politely simply to say hello. Leaders are regularly asked for advice, which in itself is the most gratifying affirmation.

As leaders, we are even praised for others' work, although our part in their accomplishment was minimal. If my softball team wins the conference, the chemistry department receives an award, or the choir presents a Christmas concert, people will congratulate me as the university president, even when I didn't have one thing to do with the specific success. And the same thing happens to you all the time.

No one has ever applauded most of the people in our ministries. Leaders hardly look up when a group begins to clap, while the people in the trenches rarely receive public recognition. But it is in our power to do something about that.

Leaders, we have enough recognition and don't need any more. We need to reverse the spotlight and not just acknowledge the achievements of those on our team but express in meaningful ways our appreciation for them as people, not only as workers.

Opportunity Leadership shifts the focus from the CEO to those who put hands and feet to the work. Although a single leader may be seen as the fulcrum—and often is the most critical touchpoint of new opportunities—a leader's effectiveness is dependent on the people around them to take seeds of ideas and nurture them to full bloom. Plus, without the people to grind the machinery of implementation, every opportunity will fail.

If you watch sports, you may have noticed that television close-ups are most often focused on the players during a baseball game, but during a football game, the camera tracks the coach. This stark contrast in the focus of attention reflects the divergence of these two leadership approaches.

As a leader, be a baseball manager who turns the spotlight around to bring attention to those working in the trenches every day to fulfill your ministry's mission. Genuinely value, empower, support, recognize, and appreciate those who will make or break the ministry's level of success. How much would you accomplish without them? You know the answer to that question.

I often remind my academic community that the most important people on campus are not the president and provost, but the plumber and electrician. If we don't have water for air conditioning and restrooms, or power for computers and lights, we are out of business for the day.

Your success as a leader will multiply when you look for opportunities to express gratitude for every employee's critical contribution. And if someone is not worthy of your praise, why are you paying them? Don't be more stingy with your accolades than you are with your money.

One specific way to appreciate your team is to personally and publicly recognize that everything they do takes longer than expected by those in leadership. What you may assume is a simple task to accomplish may have kept someone working all weekend. Putting in the effort and empathy to understand the details of team members' work is critical to success.

Long before I was a university president, I was a young youth pastor. One year, my wife and I worked from Saturday evening until dawn on Sunday to finish decorating the sanctuary in time for the first service of Advent. When the senior pastor arrived, he said, "I'm glad you were able to get that done." We were crushed. He didn't recognize what a huge job it had been. Thankfully, his wife came in not much later and raved about the decorations, saying, "You must have stayed up all night." Reporting to her that we did made it all worthwhile.

In your ministry, everything is more challenging than you anticipate and takes longer than you expect—that's the nature of organizations. Let each member of your team know that you know that. It could be the most significant affirmation you offer.

3. Be Prepared

The ultimate success of any leader will be determined by only a handful of decisions or actions. As a Christian university president, I can track it to about a dozen decisions annually that make or break our year.

Accordingly, I build my daily schedule around three priorities:

1. Don't do anything that someone else could do.

2. Move the dial every single day.

3. Be prepared for the strategic moments.

> OPPORTUNITY LEADERSHIP DEMANDS REMAINING FLEXIBLE ENOUGH IN CALENDAR, OUTLOOK, RELATIONSHIPS, AND PERSPECTIVE TO QUICKLY RESPOND TO THE CRITICAL PROBLEMS WHEN THE LEADER'S ENGAGEMENT WILL MAKE A MEANINGFUL DIFFERENCE IN THE OUTCOME.

If I don't follow the first, I can't do the second. And if I'm not effective at the second, I will fail at the third.

First, I try to keep my hands off what someone else could do effectively. I need to be doing what *only* I can do as CEO. If someone else could do it, then I stay in an advisory role.

My challenge in holding to this resolution is that I enjoy doing many of the tasks they are taking on. I like solving problems and sharing ideas, so it is tempting to jump in to help settle a conflict between two employees, teach a class on organizational psychology, or lead a mentoring Bible study group. I must resist because I make others' jobs more challenging if I pick off portions of their duty and leave them to carry the responsibility.

Leaders will frequently want to personally tackle jobs that are the charge of others on our team. But if someone else can accomplish the assignment, we need to stand back and give them room to do it. And yes, many times, you may believe you could do it better. That is because someone earlier in your career gave you the chance to learn how to do it, and now it is your turn to let them learn.

Second, for senior leaders, moving the dial every day is not measured by the volume of activity but by its strategic nature. At times, I've had a fifteen-minute phone call with a key person that moved us ahead months in our progress. I've had an occasional afternoon meeting that advanced us years forward of where we'd been had I not been engaged. Consequently, if only measured by the number of activities during a single day, my value might often appear insignificant.

There is so much that could fill a leader's day, and those married to traditional planning are caught in a quagmire of a process that makes very little lasting difference at the end of the week. In contrast, Opportunity Leadership demands remaining flexible enough in calendar, outlook, relationships, and perspective to quickly respond to the critical problems when the leader's engagement will make a meaningful difference in the outcome.

Third, leaders must be deeply engaged and widely informed. If you shadowed me for only a day or two, you'd probably label me a micromanager because I am aware of almost everything going on. My engagement seeks equilibrium to grasp the challenges without choking the organization.

I've defined my level of involvement as "micro-awareness," which has a completely different motive from that of a "micro-manager" who is seeking to control. Two purposes drive this level of detailed understanding.

It is much easier to solve problems as they are bubbling up than when they spill over. Being aware of what is in the works helps me intercept difficulties before the water gets too hot. My deep engagement is not intended to control people but to ensure that what's ahead doesn't become uncontrollable.

Additionally, and more importantly, the only way to be prepared for crucial-moment decisions is to be well schooled in the details of issues before decision points arrive. When a leader must make decisions that have a far-reaching impact on the success of the ministry and livelihood of others, it is not the time to open the book to begin learning about the topic under question.

If I don't understand our finances from top to bottom ahead of time, how could I make a decision of magnitude under the pressure of time constraints? The same is true for student campus life, academics, operations, marketing, or athletics. These require an ongoing immersion education to be ready to make the right decision or take the correct action at a critical moment.

> AN OPPORTUNITY LEADER'S LEVEL OF INVOLVEMENT IS DEFINED AS "MICRO-AWARENESS," WHICH HAS A COMPLETELY DIFFERENT MOTIVE FROM THAT OF A "MICRO-MANAGER" WHO IS SEEKING TO CONTROL.

Being prepared for the critical decision requires intense and constant preparation. The importance of this educational component of your responsibility is magnified because we never know from what arena our significant problems will come.

I've found that smaller issues will often ignite the most challenging troubles because we've not put the time into avoiding them up front. I regularly tell my team, "It is the little things that will get us."

Former Secretary of State and White House Chief of Staff Jim Baker was well known for his 5-P admonition of "Prior Preparation Prevents Poor Performance." As a meticulous planner, he depended on this mantra to guide extensive formal planning. But in a detailed study of his life, especially leading through the end of the Cold War, Baker was very much an Opportunity Leader as events developed faster than he could plan.

To be prepared for those moments when all eyes turn to you for a crucial decision or action, Secretary Baker's 5-P guidance mirrors my encouragement to be well schooled in every aspect of your ministry. Plus, your educational awareness must also include the external environment in which your ministry operates, or you will not be prepared for shifting cultural and market changes.

A critical component of your preparation requires being physically, emotionally, and spiritually balanced. When tired and stressed, all leaders make bad decisions as they navigate by emotion rather than wisdom. If worn down, our interactions with those we lead deteriorate, appearing hard, abrupt, demanding, or judgmental.

Beyond avoiding potential crashes and conflicts, new insights and inspirations bloom during times of disengagement. It is impossible to disconnect from your calling, but you can unhook from the daily grind. Purposefully detaching is the only way to keep perspective on the significant mission objectives and opportunities and not be weighed down by leadership's relentless demands. Left to its own devices, the urgent will always muscle out the important.

Being prepared for the critical moments when your ministry needs you the most requires that you are always physically, emotionally, and spiritually balanced. That won't happen without intention.

You Are Who You Are

As a university president, I've worked closely with hundreds of college coaches. They have a complex job that requires they take on the challenges of managing the egos and talents of young athletes, keep education the goal while also being determined to win games, and start fresh every year after they graduate their best players. And they do all of this while also balancing the demands of faculty, administrators, parents, and boosters.

The worst coaches I have known had one trait in common: they were attempting to emulate the style and personality of a successful coach in the "star-power" arena of their sport. On the other hand, the best coaches also shared a commonality: they were themselves and led their team in a way that fit their temperament, strengths, and outlook.

The leadership approach I've suggested in this chapter is built on encouraging independence, reversing the spotlight, and being prepared. This framework fits leaders of every style, status, and career stage. But how those characteristics get lived out needs to align with your personality, gifting, and operational mode.

You are who you are. Accept how God has made you rather than attempting to reconfigure your character to mimic someone else. Be yourself, and you will become the leader God designed you to be.

Part 3

6 TENDENCIES OF OPPORTUNITY LEADERSHIP MINISTRIES

So far, we have examined in detail six new leadership talents that are vital for capturing opportunities in ministry. When you embrace and develop these personal attributes, you will find greater fulfillment in your leadership role as your giftedness expands and your perspective shifts.

However, those six talents are not an end in themselves. The objective is to strengthen your ministry's effectiveness as a whole, not merely invigorate you as the leader. Until your ministry pulls away from traditional planning and gravitates toward Opportunity Leadership, the transformation you are seeking is still out of reach.

You can't go it alone. All your stakeholders must embrace an ethos that inspires them, collectively and individually, to choose opportunities over planning. It will take time to embolden and strengthen your team to move from defined, orderly, and pre-dictable old planning patterns. But as they begin to join with you in trusting God for opportunities, six tendencies will start to characterize your ministry's new culture.

While the specifics of your path will be unique, these six tendencies will set the overarching direction of a ministry's organizational culture to be energized and fine-tuned for Opportunity Leadership. This fresh way of operating is often unpredictable and fluid, and there is no prescient step-by-step playbook to build a culture that facilitates it. Give it time, and you will discover a passageway matching the nature of your team and the specifics of your calling.

Chapter 12

Embracing Speed

Speed wins—usually.

New opportunities are not missed because of a lack of capacity, strengths, or skills. They are squandered because most organizations, especially Christian ministries, are simply too slow to make decisions and act.

There is a golden moment in every new opportunity that will make or break the outcome. Being in the right place at the right time can't wait until you have collected all the facts, assessed the data, and equipped the team. If you can't speedily respond when presented with new opportunities, your preparation won't matter.

Think of capturing new ministry opportunities like an African wildlife photographer on assignment for *National Geographic*. There is lots of time to meticulously set up a perfect shot of zebra grazing leisurely—they will be there until you're ready. But to catch that cover shot of a lion chasing a cheetah up a tree just as the sunset is on the horizon demands being ready to act at just the right instant.

Opportunities are moving targets. You can't freeze everything until you've got all your ducks in a row to make your best decision. If that's your approach, by the time you're ready, the opportunity will have passed, and your pace will have made the decision for you.

I met with the three leaders of a technology company my university was considering partnering with to develop a short-term computer coding educational program. To get this venture off the ground, they laid out five challenges needing solutions. With two of my vice presidents joining me around the table, we heard their concerns and quickly resolved three of those problems in ninety minutes.

But then we hit a roadblock. I made a quick inquiry to see if the provost could step out of another meeting to join us—twenty-five minutes later, the fourth issue was solved.

The last problem was more formidable, and we needed the chair of the computer science department, but he was tied up teaching class through the lunch hour. I left word for him to join us for dessert, and by the time we finished, every problem was solved.

That level of speed is typical for our team, but the technology group was amazed. Their president pulled me aside to share that the previous day they went through the exact same process with a flagship state university on the West Coast, looking to begin an identical academic program. And while enthusiastic about the opportunity, their academic leaders could not compress the eighteen-month schedule required for the decisions to work through their institutional process. Our partner was quick to point out that in a year and a half, the world of computer training will have changed so much that their answer won't matter.

IF YOU ATTEMPT TO PRESS THE PAUSE BUTTON FOR NEW VENTURES, THE OPPORTUNITY WILL HAVE DISAPPEARED, MORPHED, OR DESTABILIZED BEFORE YOU FINALLY RESPOND.

Speed wins.

Every decision would be incrementally stronger if we had more time and more information, but the real world doesn't work that way. If you attempt to press the pause button for new ventures, the opportunity will have disappeared, morphed, or destabilized before you finally respond.

Faster Than a Sloth

Ministries are not slow because they are lazy. Their sluggishness is built into their organizational DNA, not their work ethic.

The adorable and lethargic sloth does not move in slow motion because of a lack of muscle mass. Instead, these intriguing animals' languid pace is the product of an extremely low metabolic rate that manifests in a low body temperature and the need for little nourishment each day.

Ministries may operate at "sloth speed" for the same reasons. The DNA of their organizational culture is built for:

- pace, not urgency
- predictability, not change
- preservation, not aggressiveness
- process, not decisiveness

I am convinced most organizations would rather live in mediocrity than grapple with a speed of change that pushes them into uncertainty.

While sharing with a potential faculty member the speed at which our university operates, the candidate recounted a story that describes higher education's DNA. The previous year he wanted to rename a course taught at his current institution—not alter the content, just change the name. He said, "After four months, my request has now gone through five committees, and I still don't have an answer." And then, reflecting in candor, he said, "I don't care anymore."

The sluggishness of higher education is not the result of subpar work standards or an absence of decision-making insight. It is built into the DNA of how colleges operate. That same slow DNA permeates the culture of church denominations, government agencies, and homeowners' associations, as well as too many service ministries and local churches. They are built for slow. Speed is not an option.

Just as DNA is made up of building blocks called "nucleotides," organizational culture is comprise of four essential components that must be re-engineered before a ministry can learn to embrace speed.

1. The DNA of Fear

Bad things happen when you go fast, right? We stress that going a bit slower is always better than faster when teaching our kids to drive. We have drilled into them that it is easier to lose control and crash when traveling at high speeds. The slower you are going, the more options you'll have in an emergency.

An inexperienced driver should always go slower, as should an inexperienced leader. That is until they have logged enough miles to know how to handle emergencies. But once we have, going too slow can be even more dangerous than too fast. Once we've gained experience, we do not need to fear organizational speed if our "vehicle" is appropriately built and prepared for acceleration.

The premier bike race, Tour de France, is never free of horrific crashes that injure or even kill a rider. A cyclist descending the Col d'Allos at sixty miles per hour is risking their life, while a Mercedes driver is relaxed at that same speed. A Formula One race car accelerates from zero to sixty in less than two seconds, which would terrify a Mercedes motorist. The racing driver could crash at 180 miles per hour and walk away, while any other motorist could never survive an accident at such speeds. And a Boeing 747 can't even lift off the runway until it reaches 180 miles per hour. None of these vehicles is fearful of speeds that fit their ability to operate.

Speed is not the issue. The construction of your ministry—how it is built and protected—will determine whether the speed is to be feared or becomes normalized. Rebuilding your organization to embrace speed reduces the level of fear and broadens your opportunity options.

2. *The DNA of Comfort*

Some ministries purposefully pump the brakes because they are comfortable. If things are going well, why add to it? The weakness of that position is the impossibility of remaining stationary. Factors will change, inside or outside your ministry sphere, and if you believe that your stability is unshakable, you will eventually be disappointed.

During the 1980s and 1990s, Blockbuster video and their 9,000 stores worldwide dominated the home entertainment business. Founded in 1985, they grew to 60,000 employees and $3 billion in annual revenues, renting video cassettes and then DVDs.[1] It was during Blockbuster's prime, in the year 2000, that its leaders met with the innovators of a bourgeoning start-up home video service. These innovators brought with them an offer to sell their company, Netflix, for $50 million—just 1.5 percent of the video giant's annual revenues.[2]

To hear the story recounted by Netflix's founder, the Blockbuster executives raised little concern that video streaming could ever threaten their business model.[3] After all, Blockbuster executives were convinced people enjoyed the family experience of coming into the store to select a movie. Plus, there was the insurmountable technological challenge of hideously slow internet. During the following decade, download speed advanced 1,300 percent. And, only ten years after Netflix's momentous business offer, Blockbuster went bankrupt.

The needs of people and the ways to serve them are ever shifting. While we can choose to resist the speed of innovation, others around us will respond to those we serve with alternatives. They will eventually be serving the clientele we assumed were solidly encamped with us.

Blockbuster is quickly being forgotten. They were comfortable, and that contentedness blinded them to the speed of change that had walked in their front door.

3. The DNA of Intimidation

In December of 2018, three universities announced launching "coding camps," the short-term technology program described in the introduction to this chapter. Those schools were Harvard, Yale, and Belhaven—not three universities you hear too often in the same sentence. While the program's market has yet to grow at the rate futurists projected, I was proud we were there on the front line of innovation with the "big guys."

Ministries are prone to shy away from opportunities demanding speed because we assume small and under-resourced ministries can't do what more extensive and name-brand operations tackle. We conjecture that whatever it takes to operate with speed is something we don't possess.

DON'T COVET YOUR NEIGHBOR'S OPPORTUNITIES. TRUST THAT GOD WILL BRING RIGHT-FIT OPPORTUNITIES SINGULARLY DESIGNED FOR YOU. AND, DON'T MISS THEM BECAUSE YOU'RE INTIMIDATED.

I'd argue the opposite position. Yes, more prominent entities have a market presence and deeper pockets, but smaller organizations are much more agile and can move at a speed big operations can't generate. We can go ahead and launch with a barebones staff, funding it as we go, while they are stuck in committee meetings.

Too many ministries don't capture opportunities because they are intimidated. Our perception has been clouded by assumptions of "we can't" rather than clarified by "how could we."

• Small does not make us inferior. We have a lean running team with fewer segmented experts and more collaborative generalists.

- Underfunded does not make us incapable. We have a bank account guided by careful choices instead of surpluses.

- Unknown does not make us ineffective. We have a deep level of service substituted for a high profile.

There is a tendency for us to look at more prominent churches, universities, or ministries and wish we were like them. Convinced we will never have their resources or reach, we cower from the speed demanded to capture opportunities. But don't covet your neighbor's opportunities. Trust that God will bring right-fit opportunities singularly designed for you. And, don't miss them because you're intimidated.

4. The DNA of Assumptions

Uber and Airbnb were not technological breakthroughs. They were the invention of those who looked beyond assumptions and considered providing the same service in ways that broke free from conformity limitations. They believed that some people would be willing to drive a stranger in their own car or let them stay in their guest room.

Assumptions constrict our future. In the mid-1940s, the president of the typewriter giant IBM predicted, "I think there's a world market for maybe five computers."[4] A decade later, the president of 20th Century Studios told stockholders, "Television won't be able to hold on to any market it captures after the first six months. People will soon get tired of staring at a plywood box every night."[5]

While laughable now, assumptions blinding us to new opportunities are just as prevalent today. As awful as the 2020 coronavirus pandemic lockdown was, it broke us free from many assumptions that restrained our consideration of new opportunities:

- Churches don't have to have in-person services to do ministry.

- Classrooms can effectively meet virtually.

- Professional sports teams can play in empty stadiums.

- Offices can function successfully with everyone working from home.

- A massive crowd is not necessary for a US presidential inauguration.

Ministries have a unique challenge dealing with the assumptions built into our DNA. Unlike a business, we must be responsive to outside stakeholders' presuppositions, not merely our own, and often those expectations are grounded in theological traditions.

From worship times to marketing, some topics are "off-limits" as we are held captive by the lowest common denominator of restrictive assumptions among our influencers. Many good ideas never see the light of day because of the misinformed conventions of a few stakeholders. In some ministries, only one major donor's assumptions will hold them back.

Every ministry is different, but as the leader, you already know the problematic assumptions held by your predictable pockets of resistance. Don't pick a fight before you must, but without some groundwork being laid, you'll never generate the speed necessary to capture significant opportunities when the time is right.

In a ministry environment, we need to always be preparing the way for change, growth, and innovation. If assumptions are not pre-emptively addressed, opportunities will pass us by before they even get a hearing.

The Pace of Speed

Three examples may help put handles on how speed works in the world of ministry.

Fast

University presidents have a peculiar and foreseeable routine when we see each other. We ask how it's going at our peer's school and always hear the formulaic reply, "We're having our best year ever. Enrollment, morale, and money are at a record high, plus the faculty love me and the football team is winning." Although, with a few presidents I've known for a long time, we cut through the PR message and talk openly.

When I came up the escalator at a conference and saw my friend Niel Nielson, the Covenant College president, I was glad to bump into someone who calls it straight. I had read Niel's letter to his constituency two years earlier, just after the global recession. I was impressed with the stewardship decisions he'd made responding to the crisis and how he communicated them transparently to stakeholders. I was walking some of that same path at my institution.

Saying hello at the conference, Niel said, "We're having our best year ever . . ." and I cut him off to admonish him to tell the truth. He said, "No, we really are! We made those tough cuts, but our donors came through, and we quickly bounced back." I was thrilled to hear of their success because Covenant is an important institution in the blend of Christian colleges and universities, and is also a sister Presbyterian college.

I then asked if he would continue the program and staff cuts he had outlined in his letter during the recession or if they were backing off those reductions. He said they would restore some, and others needed to go forward—like selling off their branch campuses. They operated branch campuses in two locations where I had always wanted to set up shop—Atlanta and Chattanooga—but resisted because Covenant College was already in those cities.

With that, my ears perked up, and hardly without thinking, I said, "Instead of selling your campuses, why don't you give them to your cousin Belhaven. We'll continue to teach it from a strong biblical perspective in the Reformed tradition." But, I was quick to add, "We don't have any money to buy them."

I like Niel because he sees the world from a kingdom perspective, and within the next few minutes, he had arranged a meeting for me with their provost and CFO, who also happened to be at the conference. Over coffee the following morning, we worked out the framework of a deal that would transfer to us their campuses and enrolled students.

The only problem was, other than talking with my provost, I hadn't tested the idea with anyone. But knowing how perfectly this opportunity aligned with our mission and expertise, I believed my faculty and board would be responsive. They were.

Over the following two months, we detailed the implementation issues of taking on this challenge, brought this opportunity to the faculty, and then presented it to the board of trustees for a final vote.

For me, the crowning moment of this experience came when presenting the idea in our monthly faculty meeting. I told this story of how the opportunity came about by surprise, detailed how well it fit with our mission, and outlined its potential positive financial impact.

I then asked for questions and discussion—but was met with silence.

Fearing I might have scared the faculty by moving too fast, I waited for someone to speak. Finally, a senior faculty member stood and said, "I just have one question. Why would we NOT want to take this opportunity God has brought to us?" I responded that I didn't know why we shouldn't act fast. The recommendation passed unanimously without further discussion.

Faster

On July 1, 2018, I received a call from a longtime friend, Michael Clifford, who is an entrepreneur in the education space, asking if my university would be interested in opening an online MBA program in China. I couldn't imagine anything more intimidating to a Christ-centered university than developing a fully online program for students half a world away, teaching a graduate-level business degree in another language, and offering it exclusively in a communist country with severe restrictions on religious proselytizing.

By this point in our journey, we had tackled a variety of opportunities. And, looking back, I could see that all that had come before was a preparation for this unique moment. We had the people, track record, and outlook to capture this opportunity, even though no other Christian university offered a degree in China.

I quickly gathered my core team to break down the options. Next, we pulled together every person on campus who had any experience working in China to gain their insights. From those meetings, we outlined a list of questions, concerns, roadblocks, and finances. We assigned those issues to various team members for operational detailing. Most importantly, we articulated the message of core values and congruency with our mission.

While they worked on the implementation side, I began to meet individually with key board members. I had two-hour one-on-one meetings with all members of the board executive committee. They raised lots of good questions and insights, and their perspectives were added to the mix. They agreed with this being a significant outreach. Of course, although not overt evangelism/discipleship, the opportunity was calling us to build friendships and trust in Christian love, just like any tentmaking missionary in a communist country.

Since this happened in the middle of summer, it was impossible to call the faculty together. Instead, we initiated meetings with key faculty influencers. Our campus had been living in a world of capturing opportunities long enough that they were not shocked, but instead worked to anticipate and solve problems.

I was especially overjoyed when I took the opportunity to our chief academic regulator, our registrar. She nearly cried, recounting that she'd always dreamed of being a missionary to China since she was a young girl. Now China was going to come to us.

Making a long story short—one month after the inquiring phone call, we signed a contract. The following month we began writing the curriculum in Mandarin. Another month later, we registered the first Chinese students in our MBA program designed exclusively for China. And only four months after that first phone call, classes began. Remember, many universities can't change the name of a course in four months, much less launch a new degree in another language.

Fastest

An unsolicited caller, who knew of our success in China, phoned to inquire about our interest in partnering in a unique academic program serving international students working in the United States. That conversation sparked enough interest to set up a conference call the following week with the educational group's founder.

My vice president working with China joined me on that call as they outlined an intricate program they had perfected at two colleges over the previous decade. They were now looking for a dozen or so universities where they could multiply their success.

The longer they talked, the more I saw this was a perfect match with our institution. Finally, not able to contain my enthusiasm any longer, I interrupted our new friend to say, "You don't need to get tied up with the different working styles and academic nuances of a dozen universities. Plus, they will be slow. You need one partner who can easily adapt to you, move fast, and is committed to supercharging this academic program. You just found that partner."

Another long story short—days later, we committed to the program and partnership. Within a few months, we hired the founder to serve with us full-time on our faculty. They did not seek additional partners after we signed on to this marvelous opportunity, and we were off and running.

Speed with a Higher Purpose

Speed is not an end in itself. Unlike a technology company or snack food brand, we aren't going fast in order to capture market share. We also aren't seeking to move quickly to muscle some other ministry out of the way, as is typical in the competition of the business world.

The commonality found in these examples demonstrates that embracing the speed necessary to capture golden opportunities is always grounded in the uniqueness of the new idea aligning with your mission, culture, and gifting. Your go-or-don't-go moment is then triggered by courage, instinct, and a gestalt understanding of your ministry's ability to execute effectively.

If you know your ministry well, embracing speed always wins.

Chapter 13

Getting Comfortable with Risk

Why are ministries incredibly slow to act when it is evident that speed is essential for capturing opportunities? Peter Drucker, the guru of modern management, summarized this challenge as a conflict between the head and the heart. He wrote, "What you have to do and the way you have to do it is incredibly simple. Whether you are willing to do it is another matter."[1] Determining a course of action and embracing the level of risk required are two completely different challenges.

Nearly everything we do in life carries with it some measure of risk. Regularly, we determine how comfortable we are with various risks. Those decisions are more emotional than cognitive and are based on feelings buried in everyone's fight, flight, or freeze predisposition.

Past experience, personal temperament, and information/disinformation mix into a blended stew that brings each person to a different point of comfort with each risk we face. For our purpose, we want to examine how ministries get comfortable with risk, but the same complexities forming risk tolerance apply to astronauts and rock climbers as well.

It is evident that if some failures don't pepper a ministry's track record, we have become far too cautious with the resources the Lord entrusted to us. After all, Jesus allowed His disciples to blunder as they learned. Paradoxically, our desire to protect limited assets is what drives us to become wary of risk in the first place. Clinging to a scarcity perspective, we may feel justified in attempting to preserve what little we hold.

HELP YOUR TEAM UNDERSTAND THAT THERE WILL BE LOTS OF FALSE STARTS, GRINDING EFFORTS, HALTED PROGRESS, AND UPS-AND-DOWNS BETWEEN EVERY GRAND SUCCESS.

Contrary to that conservative outlook, the parable of the talents in Matthew 25:14–30 makes clear that risk-takers are "good and faithful" when responding to God-given opportunities. Jesus expects us to take risks and not bury our treasure like the "wicked and lazy."

Eight specific actions will help you and your team become more comfortable with risk and, in turn, speed your responsiveness when presented with unexpected God-given opportunities.

1. Check Your Motivation

Unfortunately, some ministry leaders attempt to prove their value by projecting an "I trust God more than you do" approach when considering risk. They may genuinely believe their God-given strengths will overcome any obstacle and, thus, are drawn to a challenge. But too often, their flagrant risk-taking is motivated by the adrenaline surge that accompanies their self-aggrandizing fearlessness.

Your leadership shelf life will be shortened if you become labeled a "risk-taker" that makes everyone else nervous. Once that image sticks, it is the characteristic that will eventually get you fired. Of course, ministries want leaders to be out front. But, standing alone pushing for risk while others raise reasonable cautions is not a healthy leadership position. Predictably, the intensity of their fears will rebound in blame when the idealized future you envisioned does not materialize.

In managing risk, tainted personal motives will be manipulated by the devil to hurt your ministry. It's essential that you candidly examine your motives before considering risk. The bright light of scrutiny will eventually expose self-serving intentions. The best or worst that could happen to the ministry is the only question under consideration, not what the outcome will mean to your status.

2. Leaders Must Lead

Accepting an appropriate level of risk will not happen without a chief advocate. With your motives properly aligned, leaders must stand up and be counted at critical moments. The brink of a risk decision is not the time to hide behind boards or committees. It's also not the time to singularly muscle your way to the front in hopes of claiming all the credit if it works out. Find that appropriate leadership balance of being a vocal champion who also garners support from strategic stakeholders.

Interestingly, if it goes poorly, those who were cautious will remember you pushed for it. But lots of people will claim they were champions for the new venture if it all goes well. That's okay—it is part of leadership. What is critical is that you not wait for "groupthink" to get you to the point of taking a risk, or the opportunity will have passed.

3. A Viewpoint Is a View from a Point

Each person in your ministry has a unique perspective about risk because fear is personal. Further, it is welded to the position from which they view a potential hazard. What you may see as a great ministry opportunity, your bookkeeper may assess as risking employees' job security. Or what you may believe is innovative, a manager may interpret as discarding years of dedicated work to a project.

If the board and senior leaders' risk tolerance causes the rest of your team to become skittish, you've not yet raised the comfort level of risk that will build a platform for capturing opportunities. Just as it often works in family life, with an adventurous spouse married to one who is cautious, the spectrum of risk will range widely between individuals working together. Respect their view from their point of observation and experience.

Eventually, you must bring the whole team up to a new comfort level of risk if the ministry is to capture opportunities. You won't get everyone on board with every risk decision. If you do, it's probably not too risky. Raising the team's overall comfort with risk is good enough. Be wise and understand that it will take time. If you rush it too fast, you'll scare your stakeholders, and your path forward will become even more complicated.

4. Facts Don't Negate Fears

Those comfortable with risk often believe they can counter emotional fears with hard facts. That doesn't work when addressing risk. The chance of being killed in a plane crash is 1 in 11 million, while driving is a more dangerous trip with a 1 in 5,000 probability of being in a fatal automobile accident. But those facts don't change anyone's fear of flying. Facts matter, but they alone will not get your ministry more comfortable with risk.

Address head-on the emotional component of risk by blatantly acknowledging your understanding of the risk. The primary problem I see in ministries disconnected over comfort with risk is grounded in an assumption that the leader doesn't even see the risks that concern others. The critics have a valid point because becoming too confident about risk is risky.

If you will candidly address each of the risks and share how you've weighed them, your admission will go a long way in helping others to get comfortable with their fears. I often use best, probable, and worst-case scenarios when outlining a new opportunity and detail the risks as much as the benefits.

5. Celebrate Failure

Think back on your development as a child or younger leader. Were your greatest growth lessons learned from your successes or failures? As the great inventor Thomas Edison summarized, "I have not failed 10,000 times—I've successfully found 10,000 ways that will not work."[2] Growth comes through failures.

In contrast, ministries are quick to celebrate successes, but go to great lengths to hide failures. We act embarrassed if a venture didn't go as planned. Do we obscure the results because we are fearful others will question our spirituality, doubt our leadership ability, or hamper our fundraising? We need to mature our understanding of how God uses failure.

Teach your team to fail. Applaud them when they do, or they will never get comfortable with risk. Arguably the most creative inventor of modern times, Elon Musk, challenges his employees, "Failure is an option here. If you are not failing, you are not innovating."[3] As the leader, if you're not lifting up failure, you are rewarding mediocrity instead.

GOD IS ALWAYS PREPARING US FOR MORE. THE LORD DID NOT CREATE US TO WRITE A ONE-CHAPTER BOOK OF OUR STORY.

Don't sweat failure. Failures won't hurt you as much as you expect they will. My experience has been that every failure is the springboard for growth. I've become much more relaxed with failure through the years, but that has come only with time and experience.

6. Set Realistic Expectations

When teaching fundraising, I always remind new development officers that people like me are dangerous for their careers. We speak at conferences, dazzling the wide-eyed fundraising beginners with stories of multi-million dollar gifts. Tragically, those stories usually leave the listeners with a feeling of inferiority and bewilderment over their lack of success.

Those of us at the microphone should be telling stories about all the rejections in between each of those million-dollar gifts, not just running a highlight reel of successes.

Everything we attempt will not work as planned. Help your team understand that there will be lots of false starts, grinding efforts, halted progress, and ups-and-downs between every grand success. If they anticipate that disappointments will be mixed in with wins, they will stretch and grow.

7. Broaden Your Focus

Ministries will be jolted by failure if their focus is too narrow. If your stand-alone centerpiece project fails, it will be nearly impossible to recover. But if you are developing five new projects and three of them don't work out, you're still successfully progressing. A narrow focus will always make it difficult for a ministry to become comfortable with risk.

The wallpaper in my conference room was installed over sheet metal so that magnets will hold paper stuck anywhere on the walls. At one point, when God was bringing us a variety of new opportunities, we filled an entire wall with the new initiatives we were launching.

We would move the papers and regroup them as they shifted in priority. And then, as we got further into detailing implementation, we began removing the projects that didn't work out.

Eventually, that wall of projects was whittled down from about thirty to seven initiatives. Those that succeeded did exceptionally well. But when it was all said and done, there were more projects in the trash than on the wall. The best news is, in hindsight, we saw that in each "failure," God was preparing us for what came next.

8. Respect the Market

Christian ministries appear to be the only enterprise that assume they are protected from the influence of market forces. Yes, we are not *of* this world, but we are still *in* the world, and we can't control the economic, media, or political landscape. Influential factors beyond our control are always shifting.

In considering risk with my team, I talk about those factors beyond our control that could influence the outcome. Ministries are prone to project a stable future, and yes, most of the time, our assumptions are correct. But when circumstances around us shift, we must make changes without becoming discouraged because adjustments are forced on us from the outside.

Every year, I schedule a session to talk with my board, faculty, and staff about the potential challenges beyond our control on the horizon for Christian higher education. Some of those challenges materialize, and others don't. But by helping them think about a broader arena of our work and transparently address those issues, our stakeholders are not surprised when one of our initiatives does not go forward because of market forces beyond our control. Every time my team surveys the landscape in which we work, they become more comfortable with risk.

Starting in the mid-1990s, my university began building a ministry reach, financial model, and growing reputation by aggressively adopting alternative delivery models for accelerated education. Growing our model over a quarter-century, we launched nine campuses all across the southeastern United States, providing undergraduate and graduate degrees for students working full-time. These campuses thrived, and we served tens of thousands of students through the years.

But, by the mid-2010s, the demand for evening courses began to weaken rapidly. This market shift resulted from online education becoming more sophisticated, states offering free community college tuition, and rush-hour traffic becoming snarled in the major cities we served.

We didn't do anything wrong as a university. In fact, our exceptionally caring faculty and staff helped stave off our decline longer than most schools. But, once the financial tipping point was near, a decision had to be made to either keep pushing hard against market forces or shift course.

Watching this change unfold was extremely difficult because we had invested so much of ourselves in these campuses through the years. But when faced with the reality of the challenge, the right choice was obvious. Accordingly, we made the hard decision and closed all but two branches. Like in all "failures," God was preparing us for the next opportunities, and subsequently, other innovations gained momentum and we soon set a university-wide enrollment record.

Some might assume the branch campus model was a failure because we closed them. We don't. According to Ecclesiastes 3:1–8, that twenty-five-year run was a grand success.

For everything, there is a season:

- A time to plant and a time to harvest.
- A time to tear down and a time to build up.
- A time to scatter stones and a time to gather stones.

- A time to search and a time to quit searching.
- A time to keep and a time to throw away.

It's in the Bible

Becoming comfortable with risk is not merely an organizational management principle grounded in risk/reward ratio analysis. It is also a biblical mandate.

Opportunity Leaders have developed the talent of managed risk following the teaching of the parable of the talents in Matthew 25:14–30 that instructs:

1. Everything we have is a gift from God.

2. God trusts us more than we trust ourselves.

3. God gives us all we need.

4. God wants us to use our gifts now.

5. We can be successful, even if given less than others.

6. Being given little doesn't count us out.

7. God has His own schedule.

8. God is always preparing us for more.

9. Any effort is better than no effort at all.

10. God sees right through our excuses for avoiding risk.

11. God determines who receives the abundance.

12. God will take as well as give.

To become more comfortable with risk, study this familiar passage about a man who "called together his servants and entrusted his money to them while he was gone. He gave five bags of silver to one, two bags of silver to another, and one bag of silver to the last—dividing it in proportion to their abilities. He then left on his trip" (Matt. 25:14–15).

The money the servants invested was a gift. They didn't earn or deserve it. What God is calling us to risk is His, not ours. While our strengths embolden us in leadership, we must never forget there is not one thing we have of value in our lives that didn't come from God as a gift.

Understanding that our leadership and opportunities are gifts, it is remarkable to grasp the level of trust God has in us to be good stewards of what He has given to us. He trusts us more than we trust ourselves. God tosses us the keys to the family car and doesn't even ask where we are going or when we will be back.

The Scripture says that he divided their gifts "in proportion to their abilities" (Matt. 25:15). The man intimately knew the talents of each of the three workers. For good or bad, he could see in them what they couldn't even see in themselves and gave them exactly what they could handle. Each of the three was best prepared for success.

The parable doesn't tell us how the three servants reacted to their gift compared to what the other two received. But most likely, each was either surprised or disappointed when the gifts were handed out. What the story makes clear is that God doesn't apologize for bestowing unequal gifts.

After distributing these disproportionate gifts, the man leaves on a trip without giving his servants instructions, direction, or success benchmarks. The only way they knew what to do is because they understood the one they served. God requires that we know Him, not just work for Him.

Their master must have modeled Opportunity Leadership rather than being a plodding planner since two of the servants quickly capitalized on the moment. God wants us to use His gifts now, even though we can always contrive reasons to wait. Not being prepared, confident, or equipped are our default justifications for inaction, but they can each be traced back to being uncomfortable with risk.

Taking some risks doubled the investment of two of the servants. When we follow God's order of kingdom living, the investments pay off. But the results we generate are not the abundance God may give us in addition. That is yet to come later in the story.

My favorite part of the parable reveals that we can produce outstanding results, even if given less than others. It is fascinating that the one with the largest sum to invest didn't do the best of the group. Although two servants doubled their money, the servant with two bags had greater success than the one with five bags considering he had 60 percent less capital with which to work. If we feel shortchanged by God because we only have two bags and others have been given one and a half times as much, that doesn't mean we can't do as well, if not better.

On the other hand, look at the economics of the servant with one bag. He didn't have that much less than the servant who had the greatest success—one bag, versus two. Feeling inadequate, he was scared of risk, so he wanted to preserve what little he was given. But he could have had the same proportionate level of success if he had been more comfortable with risk.

The parable goes on to tell us that "after a long time their master returned" (Matt. 25:19). God has His own schedule. He does not operate according to the timeframe we might find appropriate and understand or how we believe He should do it. We like the timing of immediate action and reaction. Do something wrong, and you should be punished now. Do something good, and you should be rewarded now. Work hard today, and you should be paid tomorrow. While that sometimes happens, in God's kingdom the wheels often seem to grind slowly, but they do grind fine. When we assume God is ignoring us, forgetting us, or not caring about our actions, nothing could be farther from the truth. He is just waiting for perfect timing. The risks we take will pay off on His timetable, not ours.

God doesn't want us to become paralyzed by the fear of risk. For the two servants who took risks, "The master was full of praise. 'Well done, my good and faithful servant. . . . Let's celebrate together!'" (Matt. 25:21). And he also said, "You have been faithful in handling this small amount, so now I will give you many more responsibilities" (Matt. 25:21).

God is always preparing us for more. The Lord did not create us to write a one-chapter book of our story. If we faithfully use what we've already been given, He promises to provide us with more. But if we don't, then He won't.

The "wicked and lazy" servant who was uncomfortable with risk had an entirely different experience when his master returned. The servant's decision to bury his gift was based on the assumption that his master was "a harsh man" (Matt. 25:24), which the servant then attempted to back up with a string of excuses. And I'm sure, the longer he watched the other two servants investing their gifts, the more complex and engrained those justifications became in his mind. This servant never grasped how much his master trusted him, and accordingly, couldn't trust himself even to take the minimal risk of putting the money in a bank. If you believe God is stingy and anxious to find fault, you'll never get comfortable with risk.

The master then took the money from the failed servant and gave it to the one with the ten bags, declaring, "To those who use well what they are given, even more will be given, and they will have an abundance. But from those who do nothing, even what little they have will be taken away" (Matt. 25:29).

God decides who gets the abundance. It seems to me that the servant starting with two bags was the most aggressive go-getter and should have received at least half of the abundance. No, God gives the abundance to those He wishes to bless because even giving the abundance is preparation for what God has next for us. We are responsible for using well what we have been given, but God keeps for Himself the determination of who will receive the abundance.

When considering our comfort level with risk, this parable concludes by reminding us that God will take as well as give. "But from those who do nothing, even what little they have will be taken away" (Matt. 25:29). God does not hesitate to take away our gifts, leadership, and opportunities if we are not faithful in using them.

> WITHOUT RISK THERE IS NO FAITH. AND WITHOUT FAITH, WE WOULD BE FOOLISH TO TAKE THE RISKS TO WHICH GOD CALLS US.

Risk Is Required

The Bible is a collection of stories about great risk-takers. Each of their narratives is filled with daring courage as they answer the call to embrace opportunities such as building a boat, sacrificing a son, traveling on unknown paths, facing prison, or living in exile. Hebrews 11 inspires us as a "highlight reel" of many of these heroes of faith.

But, as we are strengthened in our Christian walk because of their commonality of boundless faith, we miss part of the lesson if we gloss over their differences. They were each unique individuals who faced distinct leadership circumstances. The account includes men and women, young and old, the celebrated and the unknown.

Although unique in their calling and setting, all of these leaders shared a willingness to take enormous risks that were anchored in faith. Faith is our willingness to risk everything to trust God. "Now faith is the assurance of things hoped for, the conviction of things not seen" (Heb. 11:1 ESV).

Risk is not optional. It is required of biblically grounded leaders. Without risk there is no faith. And without faith, we would be foolish to take the risks to which God calls us.

Chapter 14

Flexing for Implementation

I t was with an enormous sigh of relief that I signed stacks of legal documents to secure our first comprehensive bond issue, enabling the university to borrow $8.9 million for the construction of new revenue-generating facilities. With the last signature, locking us in for fifteen years of fixed payments, I finally relaxed, believing our long-term path was set.

Celebrating with one of my financially astute board members, I commented on the pleasure of having assured predictability. Laughingly, he said, "Oh, you'll never see the end of this note because it will be refinanced in just a few years." While I didn't want to argue with him, I couldn't have disagreed more. During that financially pressured phase, we had worked tirelessly for a year to bring together a consortium of banks to loan us that much money and stretch the loan's length to make the payments more affordable.

God had given us an opportunity. We moved fast, got comfortable with the risk, and then implemented it to a "T." We were set.

My hope for stability was naive because the board member's prediction was right on target. The world changes too fast for anything to be "locked in." As he projected, it was only three years later that we wanted to add another construction project. And, following that, we refinanced four additional times during the fifteen years I assumed our path would be cemented.

The future we envision at the launching point of a new initiative is, most likely, not how things will turn out as the dream grows into maturity. As we take off toward an opportunity, leaders must learn to think on their feet to continually adapt as a project unfolds.

When it comes to doing this, it's helpful to think about leaders in both the traditional planning model and the Opportunity Leadership model as aircraft pilots. If put in a plane's captain's seat, their approach could not be more different:

- Planning leaders imagine their responsibility similar to that of a jumbo jet pilot. They meticulously plan every aspect of pre-flight and put enormous energy into getting the massive craft off the ground. But once airborne, they expect to engage autopilot for most of the actual flying time.

- Opportunity Leadership puts us in the cockpit of a fighter jet, where constant attention and adjustment are demanded. Strap in, because the takeoff will probably be the most predictable portion of your flight to seize opportunities.

Unlike the hoped-for specificity of traditional planning, Opportunity Leaders outline a generalized direction to get moving and build a flexible organizational culture willing to adjust as the journey progresses.

Framework for Flexing

I wish I could precisely prescribe how to change and adjust as you begin to execute the work required to capture a new opportunity. I can't—because there is no formula for flexing. Every ministry, leader, board, team, and project is distinctive. Every stage of an opportunity is different, and how it intertwines with other priorities adds layers of complexity to how you handle adjustments. The length of your tenure, track record, level of trust, and quality of your core team all make your situation unique. Plus, your successes or failures of the past will open or restrict the range of course modifications to be considered as your implemented plan develops.

Instead of a formula for flexing, I suggest a framework that transposes into any setting and at any point in the implementation of any opportunity. Eight principles will provide ballast as you encounter the turbulence generated by implementing a new venture. While circumstances will be ever-changing, these core implementation priorities remain constant. Valuing these ideals will generate the strength needed during the unpredictable unpacking of an opportunity. In focusing on these eight objectives, you'll find stability in your flight into the unknown.

1. Follow the Money

Those who believe money is the "dirty" part of organizational leadership don't understand that money is your most immediate, tactical, and measurable barometer during storms. Like the stock market is a leading indicator of the economy's future, anticipating revenue and expense trends will reveal problems before you see them manifest in the deterioration of a ministry initiative.

Don't be satisfied with merely tracking budgets, but learn to build robust projection models that anticipate where you are headed financially, not just where you currently stand. Develop a reliable set of dashboards. If you don't have that expertise in-house, find a board member or consultant to build the fiscal models. A gifted financial analyst is worth their weight in gold.

In addressing my struggling branch campuses (see chapter 13), it was a detailed examination of their revenue projections based on past performance rather than hopeful thinking that clarified the hurdles we were facing. Yes, the entire team worked hard, engaged enthusiastically, and rightfully anticipated that a turn-around would be imminent. But an in-depth look at the revenue and expenditures broken down in a dozen different ways laid bare the gravity of the future. Unless leaders play games with how to count it up (too many do), the numbers are always brutally honest.

Conventional leaders approach finances with a static view, developing a budget many months before starting an operational year and then locking it down for the fiscal year's full term. In essence, this antiquated way of operating requires that every new opportunity, employee, or partnership must be anticipated more than a full year in advance. That won't work.

Along with living closer to the numbers, Opportunity Leaders also need to build flexibility into their financial framework and put money toward activities that move the dial. They are always ready to quickly reallocate resources as circumstances change. They execute every project frugally to free up dollars for future ventures. Then, just like any investment strategy, they always stay diversified in their ministry opportunity investments.

2. Predict Trouble While Preparing for Success

I can never relax around bankers and lawyers. I love them as people, but bluntly, I'm uncomfortable with their professional outlook. They assume the worst will happen in nearly every situation. It is their job to anticipate trouble, and they are very good at it—even though the sky usually doesn't fall.

On the other hand, most ministry leaders tend to have a rosy view of every challenge and possess the confidence to tackle almost any obstacle that could be thrown in their way. Without their optimism, most new efforts would never be considered, much less get out of the starting blocks.

Visionary leaders expect every venture to become successful, while bankers and lawyers look at the same opportunity and count dozens of reasons to be hesitant going forward. Neither is wrong or right—both need the other.

Because of my bent to be endlessly positive about the future, I've learned to team with bankers and lawyers to assure I am balanced in my perspective as new opportunities are presented. Their anticipation of challenges has protected me time and again as I ventured into a new daydreamed future.

I've learned from them to predict trouble while preparing for success. In that balance, Opportunity Leadership finds an equilibrium of perspective to handle a new opportunity's volatility.

3. Get the Right People in the Right Place

While I strongly advocate speed as the default mode, hiring is the one place to slow down and take your time. The biggest headaches I've ever had in leadership resulted from hiring without investing the due diligence in understanding the person I was bringing on board.

About 95 percent of the challenges leaders face boil down to one of two problems: money or people. If you hire well, the most complex of those two problems will be minimized.

In my hiring, the essential characteristics I seek are not specific skills or track records. I'm looking for people I can trust. These individuals have a teachable spirit, a commitment to service before status, emotional intelligence, a high capacity for work, and an adventurous spirit adaptable to change. Too often, leaders become enamored with a skill set or prestigious résumé and overlook these core values.

I rarely hire for a rigid organizational chart. Instead, I look to find great people and then build jobs around them as much as possible. But even with that, there are no perfect jobs, just as there are no perfect employees (including you and me). Every job has aspects that are difficult, tedious, grinding, or boring. But the more a position can be crafted around unleashing the use of someone's unique gifting, the fewer problems you'll have in leading them.

Some of my most satisfying leadership joys have been matching the right person with the right job. It doesn't get any better than to take someone who has continuously struggled, evaluate their strengths, and move them to a position where they can flourish. Sometimes the shift in responsibilities is to make a job bigger, but sometimes the best thing you can do for someone is to narrow their focus. Occasionally, it will require pulling together parts of several assignments into a single package for an uncommonly gifted individual.

God has uniquely gifted every person He created. Instead of changing their core, identify their gifts, motivations, and unique talents, and then build a job that captures the best of their strengths. And if you're unsure of what drives your key people or candidates, use a tool like TRUMOTIVATE, a Christian-based evaluation that is remarkably accurate in identifying core motivations.

In *Good to Great*, Jim Collins advocates the critical role of fitting the right people with the right job if you're a leader committed to capturing opportunities:

> The executives who ignited the transformations from good to great did not first figure out where to drive the bus and then get people to take it there. No, they *first* got the right people on the bus (and the wrong people off the bus) and *then* figured out where to drive it. They said, in essence, "Look, I don't really know where we should take this bus. But I know this much: If we get the right people on the bus, the right people in the right seats, and the wrong people off the bus, then we'll figure out how to take it someplace great."[1]

Getting the right people in the right job at the right moment and with the right objectives does not free you as the leader to flip the autopilot switch. Instead, it empowers your team to do what they do best and shifts the implementation focus from a single leader to a team of key players.

4. Develop the Courage to Stop

Ministries are awful at bringing programs to an end. When facing a no-longer-effective project, we avoid confrontation by launching a new priority that overlaps the old one's focus instead of stopping an ineffective effort. Subsequently, we run and resource two parallel tracks attempting to reach identical outcomes. But we put ourselves in a box if we are unwilling to end an unsuccessful effort before launching a new focus. Advocating for the original endeavor while justifying the new venture handcuffs each and communicates an underlying tone of unhealthy competition.

Find the courage and tact to deal with the complexities of discontinuing initiatives that have reached the end of their shelf life. Making difficult adjustments is not simply good management; it is biblical. Jesus taught us to eliminate that which does not produce results: "So every tree that does not produce good fruit is chopped down and thrown into the fire" (Matt. 7:19).

> FIND THE COURAGE AND TACT TO DEAL WITH THE COMPLEXITIES OF DISCONTINUING INITIATIVES THAT HAVE REACHED THE END OF THEIR SHELF LIFE.

Christians especially have trouble stopping activities because at the time we launched them, we were confident God was leading us. If the Lord had once called us to this task, how could we now declare it a failure? Was God wrong?

From a narrow theological interpretation of the circumstances, giving up a project becomes nearly impossible to justify. Help your team see the bigger picture of God's work. Understanding when to eliminate ministry initiatives is as important as knowing when to begin one—and your stakeholders need to grasp this concept.

I encourage working through this principle with your board and team before you have a specific issue to consider. When real people, money, traditions, and priorities are in question, taking the big picture view becomes tougher. My board has always had the courage to launch new initiatives and demonstrates an even higher level of valor at those times we've needed to stop a program.

Most boards cannot do that without finding fault with the CEO and raising their level of caution when considering future opportunities. They need to think differently about their leader. If a board cannot trust a leader in failure, they shouldn't trust that person with success either. Ministry failure is interwoven with success (i.e., Moses, Peter, Abraham, Paul). Trust God for failures. They will be purposeful steps toward healthier future success.

5. Communicate Transparently

Communicating with complete transparency is foundational for implementing new opportunities. Unlike traditional leadership planning, we need to be sharing ideas, insights, problems, and difficulties as they percolate up, not merely announcing decisions at crucial stopping points. This level of organizational communication will take some practice. Five suggestions may help to guide thinking differently about communication within your ministry.

Develop tighter messages. In planning a communication message, start by precisely defining the action you need from your audience. With your objective in mind, consider how you could explain the issues more understandably. Most leaders "wander" too much and, in doing so, confuse their audience. If you could craft a message to share in five minutes rather than twenty-five, they are more likely to be responsive. People miss what is most important if you're not succinct.

Effective communication is about the hearer, not the speaker. If they are accustomed to only hearing your announcement of decisions, they will become confused if you begin discussing the process without first explaining your new focus of dialogue.

All stakeholders must have a venue for their voices to be heard. They need to share, but even more importantly, you need to learn from them. The outlet for that two-way dialogue is dependent on formal communication structures, which slow the process. I usually learn more by popping into various offices for a ten-minute chat than I ever do around conference tables. I invite people to stop me on the sidewalk, send an email, call my cell phone, or use a communication platform to ask questions anonymously. Make it easy and flexible for them to communicate with you in ways that match their comfort zone.

Create a culture that encourages your core team to discuss bluntly any topic. With my leadership team, our meetings are not the place to come if you are worried about your ego. We talk straight, and we have a leak-proof room. Both qualities are vital. If you only want your stakeholder to confirm your ideas, applaud your work, and reinforce your thinking, that shouldn't be too hard to come by. But what good would it do you? If your team can't talk frankly with you and iron never sharpens iron, you'll never improve and grow. If your culture is grounded in one-way communication, your God-given opportunities will be squandered because you will have traded creativity and initiative for allegiance and mediocrity.

> IF YOUR CULTURE IS GROUNDED IN ONE-WAY COMMUNICATION, YOUR GOD-GIVEN OPPORTUNITIES WILL BE SQUANDERED BECAUSE YOU WILL HAVE TRADED CREATIVITY AND INITIATIVE FOR ALLEGIANCE AND MEDIOCRITY.

In empowering the voice of your people, be sure to communicate "take-home" ideas. Behind many ministry employees is a family who must also remain committed to your mission. Share ideas in stories and metaphors that can easily be "taken home" to those who love and support your stakeholders. Use this benchmark: if your employees and friends cannot articulate the mission or a significant opportunity without your involvement, then your message hasn't yet taken root.

6. Love Administration

As we talked about earlier, "I'm a leader, not an administrator" could be one of the most misguided positions a person of responsibility could take. While leaders must lead, most of what we do is to oversee implementation. You may find your greatest fulfillment in casting vision, but even in an extensive ministry, that narrow role is only a small percentage of your contribution. The day-to-day work of administration is most of what we all do. Thankfully, I love administration, and the best leaders I know do too.

Leaders cannot divorce themselves from the operational side of a ministry if they hope to succeed. While leaders may be remembered for their advocacy of significant direction-setting initiatives, it is attentiveness to the little things hidden deep down in the administrative layers that will more likely determine their level of success.

Especially in Opportunity Leadership, guidance and engagement are vital at all stages of developing any opportunity because the vision that launches the implementation process will take many twists and turns. If a leader is unwilling to become attentive to the details, the problems will multiply.

You're not too good to get into the trenches. So get over that idea.

7. Recognize That Everything Takes Longer Than Expected

As a leader, there are many dashboards and data I'd like to have as I'm engaging with an ever-changing initiative. My requests for information are usually dropped in someone's inbox through a two-sentence email. But through experience, I've learned that sometimes my simple inquiry often requires hours or even days of work from the person responsible for gathering the information. So, I've learned to start my requests with the phrase, "If this is easy to find, I'd like to know . . ."

Go even further than respecting their time, and discover what your team does every day and how they do it. You know the big picture, but get into the weeds and become familiar with their challenges. Get your hands on it, and walk through the steps with them occasionally.

The television show *The Undercover Boss* took CEOs into the hands-on world of their employees. No matter the industry, those occupying the penthouse office were startled when they saw what it was like to work in the basement. You and I can't put on a disguise and explore undetected by our team, but we can learn enough about their work that we grasp the complexity of their responsibility.

The joy of Opportunity Leadership is that new ventures often move from concept dreaming to implementation launch almost overnight. Because of the rapid pace, leaders need to be especially careful not to expect that same speed as implementation details are put into place. Yes, speed matters, but your team can't do the impossible.

Leaders who push for speed while also appreciating the intensity of the effort necessary in the implementation will build a team ready for even more significant challenges as the cycle of opportunities expands. Everything takes longer than we expect—that's the nature of implementation.

> LEADERS WHO PUSH FOR SPEED WHILE ALSO APPRECIATING THE INTENSITY OF THE EFFORT NECESSARY IN THE IMPLEMENTATION WILL BUILD A TEAM READY FOR EVEN MORE SIGNIFICANT CHALLENGES AS THE CYCLE OF OPPORTUNITIES EXPANDS.

8. Remain Steady

Ministry organizations can weather all types of challenges as long as they trust that someone has a steady hand on the rudder to guide all through the storms. This is the "dad factor" of leadership—or "mom factor" is often better. Your team wants to know the person who has the best view of all factors is confident everything will come out all right.

Rooted in godly assurance, the best leaders are never moody, volatile, or reactionary. Their leadership looks easy because they are confident their heavenly Father is doing the leading.

God Has Equipped You for Agility

As the implementation process gets into gear, learn to enjoy the constant change and motion of executing projects driven by opportunities. In the ambiguity of how the journey unfolds, God will reveal even more meaningful ministry avenues, and you may find that your target is not what you were expecting. Keep an open mind, keep your team well informed, and watch as adjustments bring your ministry closer to God's best future.

Chapter 15

Learning to Love Roadblocks

It is an extraordinary accomplishment for any university to earn national accreditation in all four primary arts disciplines—dance, theatre, music, and visual arts. Only three dozen colleges in America work at this level. So when our school achieved this distinction as an overtly Christian university, it was an especially monumental triumph.

We never planned to develop the world's premier Christian University for the Arts. In fact, as a very practical college administrator, the arts would be last on my list if I was looking for growth opportunities. My argument would have been that the students are too quirky, classes are too small, faculty too hard to find, and facilities too expensive. Plus, for a Christ-centered institution, the arts would constantly be pushing the envelope of appropriate content and producing endless headaches.

I was wrong on all counts—except for the cost of the facilities.

The myriad of opportunities that enabled us to achieve this high-level academic standing in the arts was clearly ordained of God. Because of His leading, we are now committed to becoming a university that trains Christians to embrace the arts and redeem the brokenness in the arts for God's glory.

Everything we did in the arts started modestly, but as God brought opportunities, these programs matured beyond our wildest expectations. We launched our dance program out of a refurbished storeroom with a ceiling too low to execute dance lifts. We also started a new theatre program without a proscenium stage, operated a visual arts program without a gallery, and housed our music program in basement rooms attached to a condemned indoor swimming pool. As God opened one door after another, we walked forward with confidence that He was leading us into important new areas of service.

As these opportunities unfolded, we became convinced the arts would become our university's signature contribution to the kingdom. We could become a positive influence, offering truth, beauty, and healing to the lies, ugliness, and sickness of a world alienated from the God of creation. But that's when we hit an insurmountable roadblock. All four national accreditors began demanding that we significantly upgrade our facilities or lose the national ranking. We'd reasoned that demonstrating the arts could work with limited facilities was preparing students for the real world in which venues and studios are often makeshift and under-funded. They didn't buy that argument and wanted our commitment to building facilities meriting our academic stature.

Barricades Become Building Blocks

We didn't have to go too far into architectural planning to face the hard truth that high-caliber arts facilities were financially out of reach. Our limited pool of donors had been sacrificially generous to have made possible a new $10 million student center. On the heels of that effort, the thought of raising $40 to $50 million for these four arts was ludicrous, and borrowing that kind of money would have destabilized us.

Our opportunity-infused vision for the arts had slammed into a brick wall.

On a personal level, it was an enormous disappointment. We had embraced this bold mission, gathered the right team, risked our future by going all-in for the arts, and created something unique in Christian higher education. We'd come so far and built so much, but now we were at an apparent dead end.

That was until the phone rang a few months later.

An important friend of the school called on the Monday before Thanksgiving to tell me he had good news and bad news. He reminded me his family was selling their company and had a problem we could help solve. The previous evening, they disagreed over what they should do with the company-owned insurance policy on their father. My friend said, "We all stopped and said, 'We don't argue about money in this family, so let's just give it to Belhaven.'"

He shared the good news that the university would become beneficiaries of their eighty-year-old father's $6 million insurance policy. The bad news was that we would be required to buy out the cash value to change the beneficiary, plus make the annual premium payment.

I did a quick calculation, weighed the benefit of coming up with $500,000 now against receiving $6 million someday, and said, "Okay, we'll take the deal." "Well," my friend went on, "I'm going to give you a quarter-million, and my brother will match it, so that will take care of that buyout expense."

But he was quick to remind me that the university must pay the $180,000 annual premium, or the policy would be voided—"and Dad's in great health." That computation was more manageable. I quickly answered "yes" to the obligation. But, having fun stringing me along, my friend added, "Dad is going to give you a million dollars to use for the annual premiums, and he figures that will probably last as long as he does."

Unexpectedly, only seven weeks later, the father died. Not only did we receive the $6 million from the life insurance, but we never touched the $1 million set aside for the premium. On top of these funds, a few weeks before all this happened, the father came by my office and left a $1 million check on my desk. With that gift added in, we had $8 million from this family within a matter of weeks. And, even more astoundingly, the gifts were all without any restrictions regarding how the money could be used.

The father's wife had two great pleasures in life: dance and art. So with their undesignated gifts, we constructed, in her honor, a state-of-the-art dance and visual arts facility that has few peers in the collegiate world. Although it would have been easy for us to use that money for other needs or bank it, we knew God was blessing us because of our commitment to being responsive to opportunities.

> OPPORTUNITY LEADERS CANNOT AFFORD A SHIFT BACK TO THE TIMIDITY OF A PLANNING MODEL AT THE EXACT MOMENT GOD DOES THE IMPOSSIBLE— ALTHOUGH, I GUARANTEE YOU'LL BE PRESSURED TO DO SO.

The remarkable gift catapulted our dance and visual arts programs to the highest levels, but music and theatre were still confined to derisory facilities. We desperately needed a significant performance and rehearsal venue, but the construction cost was projected to be $30 million.

I went home early after an especially discouraging meeting with the architect. But just two blocks from campus, I felt impressed by the Lord to pull into the parking lot of a church near us. It is important to understand, my spiritual life is not guided by moments of "impression," so this impulse was entirely out of character. But I knew I had to stop.

This church was a commanding tall-steeple brick building, set high on a hill with a large sanctuary and an extensive educational wing. I rarely saw activity at this church, so I never noticed it much, even though it was within easy walking distance of our campus.

About four in the afternoon, I pulled into the church parking lot, found the pastor, introduced myself, and said, "You don't know me, and I don't know you, but I want to buy your church." He laughed and quickly responded, "It's not for sale." And I admitted, "I don't have any money anyway."

After a brief tour, I'd never seen a facility so ideally designed as a collegiate arts center. The church had a gym that would make a perfect black-box theatre. Their daycare, with laundry and a high-powered ventilation system, was ready to become a costume shop. For the music side of our needs, the church parlor was an archetypal recital hall, and a long series of 1970s-style small Sunday school rooms were ideal music faculty studios. The crown jewel was their 1,000-seat sanctuary, with remarkable acoustics encased in the most beautiful academic-style stained glass windows I could imagine.

While I could envision the church as in nearly move-in condition for our theatre and music programs, the pastor was adamant the building wasn't for sale. But when we discovered a common spiritual heritage hidden deeply within family roots of the Wesleyan tradition, we began a friendship that even included me preaching their fall revival to the small congregation that had dwindled to only twenty-five regular attenders.

In the coming weeks, their leaders began to entertain the idea of selling the building, although they were crystal clear that a sale was impossible for at least a decade. But a multiplicity of opportunities shifted the climate and deepened our relationship, and seven months later, the university owned the church.

Even with significant renovations and upgrades, we paid about ten cents on the dollar for what it would have cost to construct a new venue. When detailed out, we discovered it was just about the size facility we wanted to build if we'd had $30 million.

My favorite part of the story occurred after the first service was held in the sanctuary we began using as our concert hall and chapel. I'd invited the church's leadership to be with us that day, and with every seat filled and students sitting on the floor, we had a wonderful time of worship and celebration. The chairman of the church board had tears in his eyes after the benediction as he told me, "For thirty years, I prayed God would fill this church. I just never expected it to happen this way."

In God's grand plan, the Lord designed that church facility as an arts center and let that congregation use it for three decades until the university needed it most.

Critical Crossroads

Dead ends should not be the time to charge ahead with renewed determination to bore through a hard-stop challenge for opportunity-driven leaders. Yes, many challenges do call for our grit to persevere when the going gets tough. But those obstacles are different from roadblocks. If you're pressing too hard to contrive a solution instead of trusting God for opportunities, you won't see the difference, and the results could be catastrophic.

> GOD CAN USE A ROADBLOCK TO REDIRECT US. A HALT IS NEARLY ALWAYS GOD PROTECTING US FROM MAKING A COSTLY MISTAKE.

Because of the forced polarized choice of pushing through versus trusting and waiting, roadblocks will be your most discouraging and exhilarating times—all in one. Our arts facilities' story is one of those times when God brought about the impossible in response to a dead end. But I've had many more experiences of a roadblock being used by God to redirect us. A halt is nearly always God protecting us from making a costly mistake.

Roadblocks also have a purpose beyond stopping your momentum. They are always times for significant examination. If we get so caught up in intensely solving the problem, we will miss the message God may be sending. Roadblocks are not just operational junctions, but spiritual junctions as well. They demand that leaders bring themselves and their stakeholders back to the core questions of who we serve and why we serve. For us, it was a time to renew our understanding that working at high levels in the arts was God's plan, and it was His problem to solve if we were going forward.

And then, since God had our undivided attention with this roadblock, we needed to pause to learn what God was telling us:

- Was not having top-quality facilities God's way of redirecting our service away from the top tier of the arts?

- Did the Lord need to make changes in our team before we were ready to move to a new level?

- Were we getting too proud of what "we had accomplished" and not giving God the glory that should have been all His?

- Was this focus in the arts just for a season, but now it was time to let it go?

- Were we just to wait and trust Him for solutions?

In our case, all those questions were applicable at some level, and the roadblock gave us the hard stop we needed to reexamine priorities and reground our commitment to trust God completely for the outcome.

The Lord doesn't allow a roadblock to fall into your path without a purpose. We are assured, "God causes everything to work together for the good of those who love God and are called according to his purpose for them" (Rom. 8:28). So when your journey comes to roadblocks, that hard stop should trigger three responses.

1. Examine Success

I've been privileged to be involved in building numerous campus facilities. For universities, construction is always a visible measure of success that adds value far beyond additional square footage. But I never lose sight of the fact that everything we've worked so hard to build will eventually be torn down. Buildings are depreciated on a balance sheet because they have a shelf life. Maybe they will last seventy to eighty years or, if well maintained, a building's functional life might extend to one hundred years or somewhat more. But at some point, a future president of my university will celebrate the day a bulldozer demolishes what we've worked so hard to build so that they can construct something new in its place.

Solomon was the greatest builder of the ancient world. He spent twenty years building the temple. Plus, he built towns, parks, vineyards, orchards, supply centers, chariots, and an army. "He built everything he desired in Jerusalem and Lebanon and throughout his entire realm" (2 Chron. 8:6). Although remembered today as a standard of wisdom, Solomon's story did not end well because he began to measure his worth through his ability to build rather than examining success through the eyes of God. One of the wisest men that ever lived didn't listen to his own advice chronicled in Ecclesiastes 2:4–6, 9–11:

> WHEN MOMENTUM IS HIGH AND ACCOLADES ARE COMING, ROADBLOCKS BECOME A CRITICAL TIME TO EXAMINE SUCCESS AS DEFINED BY JESUS: "DON'T STORE UP TREASURES HERE ON EARTH."

I also tried to find meaning by building huge homes for myself and by planting beautiful vineyards. I made gardens and parks, filling them with all kinds of fruit trees. I built reservoirs to collect the water to irrigate my many flourishing groves. . . . So I became greater than all who had lived in Jerusalem before me, and my wisdom never failed me. Anything I wanted, I would take. I denied myself no pleasure. I even found great pleasure in hard work, a reward for all my labors. But as I looked at everything I had worked so hard to accomplish, it was all so meaningless—like chasing the wind. There was nothing really worthwhile anywhere.

Doesn't that sound like it came from modern-day headlines, reflecting on the work of too many well-known Christian leaders who have crashed and burned because they proudly blasted through roadblocks to achieve worldly success, rather than measuring their contribution in terms of eternity? When momentum is high and accolades are coming, roadblocks become a critical time to examine success as defined by Jesus:

> Don't store up treasures here on earth, where moths eat them and rust destroys them, and where thieves break in and steal. Store your treasures in heaven, where moths and rust cannot destroy, and thieves do not break in and steal. Wherever your treasure is, there the desires of your heart will also be. (Matt. 6:19–21)

Roadblocks are a gift from God to force us to pause and examine our standard of success.

2. Lighten Your Grip

Traditional leaders are expected to control the environment around them and the actions of the team executing the plan. In contrast, Opportunity Leadership demands control be held loosely because so much remains uncertain when trusting God for the opportunities for the path forward.

Roadblocks trigger high anxiety levels in most leaders because their worth to the ministry is traditionally measured by their ability to exercise firm control when facing internal or external challenges.

A light grip is counterintuitive to our natural reaction to exercise tighter control when facing an impasse. But, especially when hitting roadblocks, a tight grip will make an intense challenge even worse. Learning to lighten, rather than tighten, your grip when roadblocks hit is a learned skill that requires discipline.

If you're a golfer, you'll understand this illustration. The key to hitting a good golf shot is to hold the club loosely in your hands like you're gripping an egg, not a titanium rod. Maintaining a light grip is not easy to do when you want to hit the ball hard, or you're upset because your last shot went into a lake.

Two actions will develop a light grip and avoid your natural response to take even firmer control of the club. First, focus on lightening your grip. You're going to squeeze too hard unless you purposefully regulate your response. With that objective fixed, second, control your emotions to ease the tightness in your hands. Fortunately, in golf, just like leadership, when you've done it successfully enough times, a light grip becomes a natural response, rather than having to deliberately focus on it during times of tension.

Learning to live with the ambiguity triggered by roadblocks is a critical skill of leaders, but unfortunately, it takes time and practice. With experience, investment in a trusted team and continual reliance on the promises of God, Opportunity Leaders learn that both God and time are on their side, and assurance is substituted for anxiety even as ambiguity levels rise.

3. Embrace Complexity

Wouldn't it be nice if leadership fell into the tidy boxes that formal planning has taught us to expect as the fruit of our labor? The benchmarks would all be hit right on target. The team would be experts while modeling ideal collegiality. Everything would happen on time, and most importantly, the outcomes would be big, bold, and singularly focused.

As recounted earlier in this book, my breaking free from traditional planning was a long and arduous journey because I didn't have a new model to follow. But even now, when facing roadblocks, I tend to be drawn back into the old planning model of simplifying the issues, focusing on the ultimate outcome, and ignoring complexity.

But organizations, problems, and people are all complex. They are never simple.

Inappropriately, during challenging times, leaders want to be seen riding the crest of the wave of a big vision, rather than appearing to wallow in the mire of complexity. Taking that "above it all" position might buy some breathing room, but it only makes the situation worse.

Nothing can live up to the simple straight-line perfect solutions projected by a formal plan, as we've discussed. Accordingly, when roadblocks bring your momentum to a halt, the temptation to project a simplified path forward must be avoided.

Embracing complexity is required of leaders during the toughest times, even though our business, political, and even church culture has conditioned followers to anticipate their leaders will magically project simple solutions to address even the most compound problems. The complexity of health care, social security, racial tensions, wage gaps, or international relations cannot be explained to the masses in sound-bite answers. And neither can solutions dealing with evangelism strategies, community housing, quality education, or church administration. But simple solutions are expected of leaders, and if we take that bait, our promised solutions to complex issues never measure up to our one-dimensional rhetoric.

Roadblocks are extraordinarily tough times for ministries. The choices will be multidimensional, intertwined, emotion-inflamed, and time-compressed. Leaders need to embrace this complexity while also teaching their stakeholders to relax in those tensions. These are times to wait for God to work in His way and at His perfect pace.

Roadblock Rejoicing

These three counterweights to the fight, flight, or freeze instinct that are triggered when we hit roadblocks not only help us find God's solution, but allow us to enjoy the majesty of our journey with the Lord. Even when dealing with overwhelming roadblocks, it is always a good day walking with God.

Chapter 16

Realigning Focus

There will be occasional times of stillness when your singular focus will be questioning when, or even if, God will bring another opportunity. But more often than not, when the momentum of Opportunity Leadership fully engages, your focus will be frayed as multiple projects compete for your attention.

During one of those chaotic periods, I outlined for my board the variety of new opportunities on our plate. In attempting to graphically illustrate the simultaneously undertaken initiatives, I presented a circle of bent arrows linked to a common core. From the source of all the arrows, I displayed our mission as the root of each project.

Our board chair cleverly pronounced the swirl of opportunities "The Tornado Plan" because it resembled a weather map when projected on the screen. More aptly, amid the tumult of opportunities we were juggling, our eyes were darting like tornado watchers monitoring swaying trees, flying debris, intense lightning, and shifting winds. With a swarm of ventures competing for attention, we had to learn how to fix our focus on what matters most during the intensity of a storm—protecting people, not property.

During this period of rapid change, we began learning to realign our focus. Of course, staying agile is essential in being responsive to a variety of problems and timely decisions. But as the matrix pulls our attention from one urgency to the next in an attempt to keep everything equally secured, we tend to lose our concentration on what matters most.

While moving fast, flexing, and adjusting to roadblocks, the lasting significance of your work will be found by realigning your focus. Develop the discipline to favor three aims:

1. Focus on outcomes, not just operations.
2. Focus on people, not just problems.
3. Focus on agitators, not just the agreeable.

As workloads intensify, deadlines loom, and projects become complicated, we will tend to become frazzled rather than focused. Opportunity Leadership's shifting nature demands that we concentrate on these three values that transcend the push-and-pull of the urgent.

1. Focus on Outcomes, Not Just Operations

Our mission moves from prophecies to practice in ministry as we pour ourselves into the operational machinery that brings life to programs, projects, and priorities. Rightfully, to advance ministry work forward in effective and timely ways, most leaders live, eat, breathe, and sleep their responsibility. Despite our best intentions, there are few boundaries between our work and personal lives because ministry leadership is all-consuming.

Full investment in your ministry is fundamental if you expect God to bring opportunities. If you're not entirely bought in to the calling of your assignment, then get out of the way and let someone else do it. From your perspective, what God has entrusted to your care should be the most crucial thing in the world. If you're not convinced of that, you surely can't ask donors to support your work, and more importantly, you shouldn't ask God to bless it.

But a commitment to calling is not often the problem of leaders. Our issue revolves around this challenge: targeted outcomes become obscured when we are focused on operations. The relentless urgency of operational demands will take as much from us as we will give. But without a deliberate realignment, keeping our ministry's mechanism running smoothly will make us lose sight of why the engine was originally built. As a result, "our program, goals, and initiatives" overshadow the needs we are attempting to meet. We haven't missed the mark; we have simply had our attention, energy, and message shifted from the main thing to our thing.

Let me give you an example. A medium-sized denomination invited me to help craft their annual Thanksgiving offering. Studying patterns from previous years, they usually highlighted their missionaries, church planting, educational, and other denominational work in one country where they served. In response to a compelling overview of their operation, members were asked to fund those activities. It was a typical fund-raising pattern of "give to support what we do."

Instead, I challenged them to build a message around the outcomes they were attempting to achieve through their mission efforts in the featured country. We highlighted the population's needs and not just those attending their churches. We also profiled the political, economic, cultural, and educational challenges, as well as spotlighted the spiritual structures, religious history, and unreached groups across the country. As a result, the Thanksgiving message focused on the needs of people, not on the denominational programs.

We then closed the appeal with a brief "in response to these needs, this is what we are doing" request. We summarized the denomination's missionaries, church plants, educational services, and other ministries. Most importantly, we stressed how people's lives were changed because of those activities. The message was all about outcomes, not operations.

Stakeholders want to make a difference in the lives of the people we are called to serve. They don't want to give to our "office," "program," or "goal," but instead, they want to give to be part of a solution to a problem. With this shift in focus from operations to outcomes, that Thanksgiving offering raised three times as much as the previous years.

When you realign to focus more on outcomes rather than operations, your external constituency will increase their giving. But most importantly, your ministry employees will be energized for their daily tasks when you keep their focus on outcomes rather than unrelenting operational demands.

> STAKEHOLDERS DON'T WANT TO GIVE TO OUR "OFFICE," "PROGRAM," OR "GOAL," BUT INSTEAD, THEY WANT TO GIVE TO BE PART OF A SOLUTION TO A PROBLEM.

To me, there is no higher satisfaction in leadership than seeing the mission permeate the daily work of every employee. One day, as I was walking across campus, I saw two of our maintenance staff standing in a five-foot-deep hole with water up to their knees. They were obviously repairing a water leak. "What are you guys up to?" I asked while trying to keep mud off my shoes. "We're educating students for the Lord," was their quick reply. They got it. Their calling wasn't to operations but outcomes.

When consulting with ministry boards, my opening question often shocks: "What difference would it make if you went out of business?" Predictably, they will highlight the breadth of the work they have established, the number of people served, the maturity of their operation, and the strength of their resources to assure stability. All of that is laudatory.

A follow-up question probes, "Could some other ministry do it better?" Their response refines their unique value, touting the giftedness of their employees and their programs' strengths. Plus, they will usually trace an institutional history that differentiates them from other similar ministries. Thankfully, they will make a strong argument for being irreplaceable.

This line of questioning helps ministries dig deeply into their calling, but we must reach bedrock. No matter how magnificent and magnanimous our operations might be, the outcomes are calling. The question is not, "Do we excel at what we do every day?" Rather, the issue is, "Does it make any difference?"

Our final exam comes long after graduation for a Christian university, best measured at the fiftieth-anniversary alumni reunion. A church's impact is assessed by community and family ministry that takes place all week long and not just in attendance on Sunday. The outcomes question is answered uniquely by every ministry, but if not asked with brutal frankness, our focus will become valuing our operations instead of meaningful outcomes.

Especially as opportunities multiply and the swirl of activities accelerates, responding to operational demands will pull our focus away from the eternal to the urgent. Instead, stay disciplined in realigning your focus to "think about the things of heaven, not the things of earth" (Col. 3:2). Lead your team to make this adjustment in their focus. It will make all the difference in their outlook, success, joy, and impact for the kingdom.

Every day when they come to work in a ministry, they are not coming to a job. They are coming to a God-given opportunity to impact somebody's life in a way that will be transformational. Each day could be an occasion to clear a roadblock for somebody who feels overwhelmed. At any moment, a door may open to help someone in despair find hope. Or an unexpected encounter could lead the way for someone to reorder their life.

In whatever the assigned task, for those working in a ministry, God is looking over their shoulder, whispering, "I'm going to send somebody to you today who really needs you." What a moment! Operational needs may demand 90 percent of your time, but don't let those demands consume most of your focus. We have joy going to work if we focus on outcomes instead of operations.

2. Focus on People, Not Just Problems

Sticky challenges consume leaders' lives—this is what we do. Most effective leaders tend to love solving problems. We find the riddle in them fascinating, and discovering workable solutions is satisfying. Accordingly, successful leaders are drawn to problems and dive in headfirst to solve them.

Because there are not enough hours in the day, problem-solving leaders have learned to juggle multiple challenges simultaneously by working efficiently. When the pressure is on, they are comfortable with "bottom-line" discussions that cast aside all entanglements to focus on solution options. When the schedule is in overdrive, they solve problems with quick stand-up meetings instead of hour-long chats.

In the urgency of addressing challenges, our laser-focus on problem-solving can run roughshod over the emotions and worth of the people we serve. Most critically, when immersed in seeking solutions, we tune out the personal interactions that will become our life-blood for the future. It's easy to forget that:

- *Sometimes* people need to tell their story, even if you know the answer after the first few sentences of their explanation.

- *Most times* asking about their kids and spouse is a lot more important than knowing about their work.

- *Every time* caring about who they are matters more than what they do.

As your pace quickens and the variety of projects accelerates, the likelihood of slighting people dramatically increases. So you need to keep in focus two axioms of ministry relationships.

First, opportunities are rooted in friendships. God has blessed me with more new opportunities than I could ever imagine. In reflection, every one of them came as the result of a friendship. Yes, some opportunities will be spawned as you refine solutions, but nearly every new opportunity will come about because the Lord brought people together at the right time and place.

One of the little-known secrets of higher education is that people do not go to Ivy League schools for the education. Of course, it is a world-class learning environment, but students primarily go for the friendships they will establish. Although we may disagree with the premise, at the top levels of the political and business arenas, who you know opens the door to power and money, not your ability to solve problems.

> PARADOXICALLY, IT IS IN MANAGING PROBLEMS WHERE A LEADER'S VALUE IS MOST IMMEDIATELY JUDGED, BUT IT IS IN THE RELATIONSHIPS WHERE LASTING LEADERSHIP FLOURISHES.

Ministry operates on a different currency, but relationships are also the engine that drives our expansion. One of the great cooperative ministry efforts of past years has been Table 71, a loose association of Christian ministries committed to evangelizing the world's unreached people. That momentous effort came about because a group of friends sat together at Table 71, among the one hundred tables set up for discussion groups at the Amsterdam 2000 evangelism conference sponsored by Billy Graham.

Great leaders have lots of friends. It is common to all of them. And if you evaluate failed ministry leaders, they focus on being magician problem solvers but systemically create conflicts in their friendships. Subsequently, their circle of relationships tightens, and they burn their bridges behind them after personal confrontations. Eventually, their opportunities dry up.

Paradoxically, it is in managing problems where a leader's value is most immediately judged, but it is in the relationships where lasting leadership flourishes.

Second, transactional ministry relationships are limiting. God has room to work when we invest in relationships without knowing where a friendship might take us. Unfortunately, too many leaders are responsive only to those from whom something could be gained from the connection. We must do better because transactional relationships are not the pattern of Jesus and produce a selfish focus that narrows ministry opportunities. This is a challenging shift for leaders because we have been trained to focus on direct and measurable returns from our investments.

Dr. Billy Kim is a close personal friend and one of the world's most deeply respected Christian leaders. He has remarkable influence at the highest levels of the church, government, and business, and builds the kingdom with a humble spirit and a passion for evangelism.

But if not for the goodness of an American soldier, Dr. Kim might not have found Christ. And he also wouldn't have become the pastor of a 15,000-member church, leader of Far East Broadcasting–Korea, president of the Baptist World Alliance, friend and spiritual counselor to world leaders, and evangelist of the gospel to millions of people.

After Billy Kim's small school was bombed during the early days of the Korean War in 1950, he decided that "working for an American soldier would be the next best thing to getting an education." In exchange for Hershey bars, C-rations, and cigarettes that his mother would sell on the black market, Billy cleaned soldiers' tents, gathered their firewood, and made sure their stoves stayed stoked.

Billy didn't speak any English, other than curse words he had learned from American GIs. But because of his work ethic and bright personality, the Korean teenager attracted the attention of Sgt. Carl Powers, who started teaching him English. And as a seventh-grade teacher at home in the United States, Carl's concern for Billy grew from superficial intrigue with a Korean personality into genuine love and brotherhood.

With Billy's country being devastated by war, Carl wanted to find a way to save this bright boy from the chaos. He knew of Billy's desire to become a politician, so Carl began to make arrangements to help the teenager get an education in the United States. In turn, Billy could help rebuild Korea after the fighting.

Using his limited military and teaching income, Carl provided a way for Billy to come to the US and enroll at Bob Jones University in South Carolina to complete high school, college, and graduate school—with Carl paying the tuition, room, and board all the way through. One night while enrolled as an undergraduate, a fellow student led Billy to the Lord, explaining John 3:16.

The most fascinating aspect of this saga is that Sgt. Carl Powers was not a Christian when he sent Billy to America for an education—and Carl wasn't aware the university was a faith-based school. But after Billy found Christ, he shared the good news with Carl, and years later, baptized him in the River Jordan.

Carl and Billy's story offers astonishing insight into how the Lord plans far beyond what we can see or understand at the time. Carl never had much money but chose to invest in a young teenager's education. Through Carl, God was preparing Billy to reach millions of people with the gospel. Their friendship is a magnificent demonstration of how God can use our investment in people if we are not looking for anything in return.

3. Focus on Agitators, Not Just the Agreeable

In ministry, nearly all the people in our orbit are supportive, encouraging, and agreeable. The bond of Christian love tends to overlook shortcomings, although a few people in the church can be especially harsh, judgmental, and unrelenting. It is a heavy two-edged sword, with the few weighing us down more than the multitude.

Maybe it's because we are unaccustomed to aggressive confrontations that most ministries have not developed a positive framework for successfully working with agitators. We are not a business, but we can learn much from the arena that studies agitators in detail regarding negative reviews.

The White House Office of Consumer Affairs reports that dissatisfied customers typically tell nine to fifteen other people about their experience; some tell twenty or more. I would imagine that in Christian ministry, those numbers would be even higher because our work is deeply personal.

It is alarming that "it takes roughly 40 positive customer experiences to undo the damage of a single negative review."[1] This is why Truett Cathy, the founder of Chick-fil-A, taught, "Never lose a customer."[2] His business principle was grounded in Jesus' teaching about one lost sheep.

Understanding what is at stake, businesses caringly respond to agitators, finding that seven out of ten consumers changed their opinion about a brand after the company replied to a negative review. Further, when a business replies to at least 25 percent of their customer reviews—especially the negative ones—on average, they earn 35 percent more revenue.[3] The business world has learned it is crucial to engage agitators, while, too often, ministries tend to discount them.

In ministry, there will always be agitators. I'm convinced the Lord uses agitators to keep us humble and gracious. Plus, as in business, they reveal weaknesses in our work or communication. They are good for us, not an evil to be expunged. Moreover, they are our best opportunity to practice what we preach.

Agitators have become more aggressive because email tolerates higher levels of intensity. When agitators attack, teach your team to be responsive to the person before fixing the problem. Our natural reaction is usually to resolve the issue quickly, hoping the dissenter will be muzzled. Of course, a solution is critical, but if you show care for the person rather than just the problem, you'll understand the issue at a deeper level. So before you write back, remember that the person you are responding to is deeply loved by others, and those people will read your reply too. Write the email you would like to receive. Better yet, write the email you hope your child would receive. Best of all, pick up the phone when tensions are high.

Empathize with agitators' frustrations and urgencies. Learn the context of their problem, and repeat it back to them to confirm you've heard and grasped their issues. Understand enough to support their effort to overcome challenges, rather than becoming another stumbling block in their journey. Assume you don't know their whole story; if you did, it might bring you to tears. Extend the grace of God and let it fill in the places of hurt you will never see. Most importantly, serve agitators until you've changed the narrative. Invest in a relationship with an aggressor until the message they share with friends shifts from "they hurt me" to "you won't believe what they did to help me."

> TOO MANY LEADERS LIVE LIKE A LONG-TAILED CAT IN A ROCKING CHAIR FACTORY THAT HAS BEEN UNEXPECTEDLY HURT TOO MANY TIMES.

Also, realize that sometimes you just need to apologize. There will be times we miss it in ministry and, in those times, just apologize without qualifiers. It's amazing how far an apology will go to help mend a relationship and change the narrative.

Jesus taught His team a framework for dealing with agitators:

If a soldier demands that you carry his gear for a mile, carry it two miles. . . . love your enemies! Pray for those who persecute you! . . . If you love only those who love you, what reward is there for that? Even corrupt tax collectors do that much. If you are kind only to your friends, how are you different from anyone else? Even pagans do that. (Matt. 5:41, 44, 46–47)

Although repeatedly taught, our Lord's disciples could not put the lesson into practice in the heat of the moment. Instead, when Jesus was being arrested, His followers took out their swords to fight. At that moment, when tensions were the highest ever among the disciples, Jesus de-escalated the intensity by responding in grace, healing a wounded agitator, and telling His disciples to put their weapons away. The gentle, graceful, and loving response of Jesus to agitators clarified His mission more than His words ever could.

Productive, Not Protective

Too many leaders live like a long-tailed cat in a rocking chair factory that has been unexpectedly hurt too many times. They are anxious about everything around them because they don't know from which direction the next attack will come. In response, their leadership mode becomes protective rather than productive.

Focusing on outcomes, people, and agitators will realign your priorities and outlook, and in turn, your anxieties. When you can lift your focus beyond operations, problems, and only the agreeable people, you will elevate your perspective of the work as a whole and discover your best opportunities for strategic leadership. In making this shift, you'll gain a stronger grip on the priorities that will best propel your ministry forward, as well as a deeper awareness of pending trouble.

Chapter 17

Being Like
Jesus, Really!

Ideally, once your ministry becomes focused on capturing opportunities rather than pushing long-range plans, your workplace
should become one angelic environment because the anticipation
of God's leading overwhelms the gravitational pull toward conflict,
misunderstanding, and style-clashes.

It won't!

In fact, relationships may get even more strained for a while
because the lines will be blurrier. And your organizational structure
will become more fluid as you shift priorities and adjust relationships
to create work teams that are responsive to new opportunities.

Frankly, even in a Christian ministry, the workplace is reminiscent of the "group projects" we first experienced in fourth grade, with
more energy given to struggling for control of the group or fighting
with those who won't do the work than in building the science fair
volcano. I've been in education my entire life. I'm convinced that
students at every level (from elementary through graduate school)
hate group projects because the focus is too often centered around
personal tensions rather than the task.

My theory is that all our bad experiences with group projects in
school have shaped the workplace in which the culture can be:

- hijacked by a few people who've become adept at getting others to carry their load
- fragmented by those who have learned to segregate themselves by leveraging expertise
- controlled by overachievers who have learned to do it all on their own while dragging the others along

While it takes workgroups to produce significant outcomes, we've learned to *work together* without always *being together* in our outlook and spirit.

Whether my educational framework theory is correct or not, it is evident that a workplace is where elbows can be thrown in gaining position, territorialism can trump logic, and the push-and-pull of the daily grind can cause people to react in overaggressive ways.

As ministry leaders who are the voice and hands of Jesus, we must create a workplace that is better—much better. To do that, let's go back to our core: our desire to be like Jesus.

Grace and Truth—That's It!

The life of Christ is so multi-dimensional, it may appear hard to pin it down to the top priorities. But the disciple John, the one who knew Him best and the one Jesus entrusted His mother to when He was on the cross, summarized the life of Jesus into two priorities: *grace* and *truth*. John wrote, "The Word became flesh and made his dwelling among us. We have seen his glory, the glory of the one and only Son, who came from the Father, full of grace and truth" (John 1:14 NIV).

> IN CHRIST, TRUTH AND GRACE ARE INTERDEPENDENT. YOU CAN'T HAVE ONE WITHOUT AN EQUAL MEASURE OF THE OTHER.

Just as Jesus was fully man and fully God, He was also fully truth and fully grace. It wasn't 50/50 percent. It was 100/100 percent. He never wavered in the truth, and we shouldn't either. He never wavered in grace, and we shouldn't either. In Christ, truth and grace are interdependent. You can't have one without an equal measure of the other.

Yet, although Jesus was full of grace and truth, when the call to arms is trumpeted in the culture, education, or preaching wars, Christians who are quick to highlight their willingness to lift up truth often appear just as anxious to downplay grace. But being an ambassador of truth alone is not being like Jesus. To be like Jesus, our focus is not truth and theology, truth and scholarship, truth and politics, truth and discipline, or truth and programs. No, Jesus was full of grace and truth.

Notice the order that John used when listing these priorities. He said, "grace and truth." He probably put grace first because the Jewish people expected Jesus to be full of truth. It was the grace that was so shocking. The path to holiness is not through truth alone. It is truth *and* grace. And unfortunately, it is easy to see the damage Christians create when their sole focus is truth, because truth without grace is self-righteousness.

What would the advance of the gospel look like if ministries, churches, Christ-centered universities, and Christian schools became as passionate about modeling grace as we are about teaching truth? With our intense arguments for truth, Christians are pushing people away from Christ because they do not live out an equally intense commitment to grace. It is time for Christians to lead with our grace, so our truth will be welcomed. If we do, we will be more like Jesus, and we will work in a thriving godly community. And more importantly, we will equip a new generation of Christians to bring hope to a hopeless world as they fully reflect Jesus—100 percent committed to truth and 100 percent committed to grace.

Grace is not a slogan, program, or annual theme for your ministry. It is living in Christ and being like Jesus. If it is not transformational, then what's the point?

As our culture continues to shift, if we don't find a deeper level of grace, we will not have the strength to take on the enormous challenges and, as the pressure from outside mounts, the tension inside ministries will accelerate. Without resolute leadership to construct a culture of grace, escalating frustrations will trigger ministry teams to turn on each other:

- When pressure escalates, emotions run roughshod over relationships.

- As the stakes get higher, emails get more accusatory.

- As the pressures mount, speculation of motives intensifies.

- When money is tight, functional silos become more defined.

- As organizational cultures shift, intractability becomes more deeply rooted.

- As demands escalate, fault-finding supplants problem-solving as the norm.

All of that will happen *unless* leaders and their ministries are committed to a culture of God-honoring grace. If we equip those in our sphere of influence to be like Jesus, full of truth and grace, they will have the strength to take on the formidable future ahead. And if we don't, and allow them to focus on only truth or only grace, we are preparing them for a hard fall.

Grace Must Be Purposeful, Practiced, and Prayerful

Writing to his protégée Timothy, Paul urges him to "be strong through the grace that God gives you in Christ Jesus" (2 Tim. 2:1).

Paul doesn't instruct Timothy to focus on preaching, prayer, giving, study, or theology—as vital as each might be. He compels him to focus on grace and to build up strength for what is ahead.

It is critical to understand the context for Paul's instruction that's essentially saying, "Right now, Timothy, before things get tough for you, build up grace in Christ as the centerpiece of your life, or you won't have the strength to handle what's coming." And for Timothy, what was ahead was seeing Paul in a Roman prison, which was a hard and horrible place.

For Paul, Timothy, and for us, the only way to manage a tough future is if grace dominates. But it will take some purpose, practice, and lots of prayer. Like Timothy, we need to bulk up in grace to have the strength to handle our ministry's future.

Acquiring the level of grace that will sustain us through times of intensity and challenge is grounded in embracing the enormity of grace given to us through Christ's redeeming sacrifice. If this grasp of grace is not our bedrock, then we'll always come up short.

There are essentially four types of people who fill up churches, including those who:

1. play around the meaningless edges of its faith because they are *bored*

2. construct their faith through comparisons to others because they are *bitter*

3. strive to be deserving by segregating theological classes because they are *tired*

4. surrender to the magnitude of God's grace because they are *strengthened*

There is little wrong with the church that couldn't be fixed by a fresh understanding of how completely hopeless, destitute, and undeserving we are without the grace of Christ Jesus—and that only through grace, given freely and without any stipulations, are we saved. Those are the kinds of Christians who clarify faith in culture rather than adding to the confusion.

Leaders must model the standard of grace that honors the Lord. If we don't push to elevate grace in our workplace, we not only lose the strength of our ministry, but we dishonor the significance of Christ's gift.

> IT IS TIME FOR CHRISTIANS TO LEAD WITH OUR GRACE, SO OUR TRUTH WILL BE WELCOMED.

How much grace should you give those who work with you when they disappoint? How much grace does Christ give us when we break our promises to Him? How much grace does He give us when we overreact, get angry, lash out, ignore, or purposefully defy Him? If Christ didn't give us too much grace, how could we possibly give too much grace to others?

Don't worry about overdoing it with grace in your ministry—you won't.

Putting Handles on Grace

Business models of the world have taught us to give grace sparingly in order to motivate and set a standard of excellence. To me, that's just heady power. Ministry leaders must reject this norm and instead become more purposeful about finding opportunities to give more grace and not less.

I won't begin to offer a comprehensive list of ways to model grace as we work together in ministry organizations, but a few handles for how grace gets lived out in leadership may trigger your thinking.

1. Minimize Power Differentials

Power differentials are built into the fabric of organizations. One person has substantial power or leverage over another because of their responsibility, experience, or personality. When power differentials are significant, our commitment to grace must be even more purposeful.

If not guarded, we could easily fall into the tempting practice of power, which focuses on others' deficiencies rather than their potential. If, instead, your outlook is dominated by grace, you might discover:

- The Peter in your ministry, who might deny Christ by the fire one night, but could be there to light the fire of Pentecost a short time later.

- The Mary in your workforce, who sometimes frustrates others for not always carrying her load, may be pursuing higher objectives.

- Joseph, the spoiled one among your workforce who expects to be pampered, might need to be jarred out of complacency and put into a place where he can grow into a great leader.

- The employee temporarily distracted by complex challenges in their personal life, could become a Ruth, who sets your ministry's standard for tenacity and devotion.

- The stammering shepherd on your team might become a mighty Moses.

- And the dreaming Noah of your ministry may be the only one to see the oncoming flood.

It is too easy to default to the efficiency of power that ignores grace. There is no doubt you could accomplish something faster and more efficiently with power, but there will be long-term costs to pay in relationships. The more power you have in a relationship, the more grace is demanded.

2. Look for the Overlooked

I usually do the grocery shopping for our house, but I was in a big hurry one afternoon and asked my twentyish daughter to run to the grocery store with me. The place was crowded, they didn't have all we needed, and the checkout lines were long and slow.

When it was finally our turn, the young woman scanning the groceries flirted with the high school football player bagging what we bought. The slower they went, the more frustrated I became until I started taking over both of their jobs to speed the process. I didn't do well at that moment and, as we finally pushed our cart to the car, I knew it.

My wise daughter rightly scolded me after we were alone in the car. And she forever changed how I see people, calling me out to say, "Dad, your generation thinks that anyone who wears an apron is there to make your life easier, and you look right past them. You don't know what a horrible job those kids have."

She was not only right, but even worse, I was horrified to realize that I never noticed that those who work at a grocery store even wear aprons.

Since that day, I watch for aprons. If a service worker is wearing an apron (in stores and restaurants), I ask how their day is going, what their plans are, and tell them how much I appreciate their help. Not only have I brought some grace to them, but more importantly, it has significantly changed me as I learned to look for the overlooked.

Giving a little time and a bit of yourself to the overlooked in your ministry and your world is not only the fullness of godly grace, but it's an essential component in building a culture of grace.

3. Don't Be Stingy

One of my friends from years back made a ton of money and gave nearly as much away. He's also an author, so when I saw he published a new book, I invited him to come to our campus to speak in chapel even though we hadn't been in contact for over a decade. He was so wealthy that I didn't even bother to send him a plane ticket, assuming he'd fly first class or in his private jet.

I was anxious for our students to learn from him. And, being a university president who often must mesh objectives, I also thought if he spent a day on our campus, he might help the university financially. It turned out to be a treat to get reconnected over dinner personally, but it was also shocking to learn that his fortune was gone and he barely had enough cash for his plane ticket for the trip. He told me about his plans to recover financially, but like many entrepreneurs, that up-and-down ride is unpredictable.

We had a wonderful chapel, and his message was right on target. It was great to renew the friendship. As I dropped him off at the airport, even though our university budget was extra tight that year, I gave him a $1,000 honorarium plus travel expenses because he seemed to be in a place where he desperately needed the money. (We usually don't pay chapel speakers.)

THERE IS NO DOUBT YOU COULD ACCOMPLISH SOMETHING FASTER AND MORE EFFICIENTLY WITH POWER, BUT THERE WILL BE LONG-TERM COSTS TO PAY IN RELATIONSHIPS. THE MORE POWER YOU HAVE IN A RELATIONSHIP, THE MORE GRACE IS DEMANDED.

Several years later, I received this unexpected note:

Dear Roger –

If my recollection serves me, your university paid me an honorarium of about $1,000 a few years ago to speak in chapel. You recall at the time I was in rough financial straits from which God has graciously delivered me. Thus, the enclosed $5,000 should repay your kindness with a bit of interest thrown in. May God continue to bless your efforts there at Belhaven.

P.S. I had second thoughts about this. So I made it for $10,000. It happens.

This incident was a wonderful reminder not to be stingy with grace.

4. Deliver Personally

The church has become overly impressed with big numbers. Sunday attendance is measured in thousands, evangelism efforts in tens of thousands, and media campaigns by millions of people reached. We have been duped into equating ministry size with ministry importance.

On the other hand, meaningful acts of grace are delivered one person at a time, and only with a significant investment on the part of the giver. For an accurate measure of importance in the eyes of God, grace beats gigantic every time.

I'm privileged to work with a grace-filled group of faculty and am amazed at the lengths they will go to help a student. Our faculty is an anomaly in the academic world that mistakenly prides itself in labeling unforgiving rigidity as academic quality. And, the story of an imposing football player with a failed academic history demonstrates the transformational power of grace when delivered personally.

Growing up, he was such a great athlete that teachers allowed him to coast through school for the "good of the team" but never equipped him with essential academic skills. Because his self-esteem was welded to his athleticism, he had little hope of a successful future outside the gridiron. So unless something dramatic happened, this young man was destined to return to a life with few options.

When he transferred into our university, one faculty member, with no interest in football, took a particular interest in him—not as an athlete, but as someone who had been underestimated his entire life. Through patiently listening to his story, which he'd never before been asked to tell, she discovered a fearsome football player with a gentle heart. And she became equally fearsome in her determination to turn his life around.

The faculty member not only guided him through her class but began tutoring him for success in other classes. She recruited other faculty to provide him extra help and pleaded for scholarships to allow him additional time for study. Most importantly, she pushed him to believe in himself and not give up on his dream of using coaching to help kids become more than football players.

Remarkably, through her efforts and a cadre of her colleagues, he finally earned the GPA required to graduate, but needed a master's degree if he ever hoped to teach and coach in his home state. Was this a dead end? The rigor of a master's degree was an academic bar that seemed impossible when the professor first met the football player. Plus, after bouncing around too many colleges, he was entirely out of money.

Our responsibility to offer grace doesn't end when we hit a roadblock.

Through a remarkable turn of circumstances, a university close to his home awarded him a full graduate tuition scholarship as an unpaid coaching assistant. He completed his master's degree with a solid GPA. Beaming with pride, he returned home to become a teacher, and coached his team to the conference championship in his first year. His life was transformed because grace was delivered personally.

5. Drain Emotions

Godly grace often evaporates when emotions intensify, triggered by conflict, deadlines, or weariness. When emotions become elevated, de-escalation should be our default mode as leaders. Whatever has someone stirred up can be worked out later when the emotion is drained from the situation. A deadline can usually be pushed back, or sometimes a time-out is the solution to the exhaustion of pushing.

When a constituent or coworker is emotionally charged and pressing, if you can de-escalate by assuring them of your desire to help them solve the problem—but build in a bit of space so you can sort it out—then you're on a graceful path.

- In times of chaos, respond with calmness.
- In times of hostility, respond with hope.
- In times of anger, respond with empathy.
- In times of exhaustion, respond with listening.

Grace is much tougher to live out when emotions are high. If grace was easy, everyone would do it.

6. Make It Pervasive

Building a transformational culture of grace at your ministry requires that grace is as central as truth. Grace is not reserved for exceptional circumstances any more than truth is heralded with caution. We must learn to allow grace to permeate every aspect of our ministry:

- Grace in uncertainty
- Grace in change
- Grace in pressure
- Grace in waiting
- Grace in opportunity
- Grace in creativity

- Grace in wisdom
- Grace in complexity
- Grace in tight budgets
- Grace in inequality
- Grace in weariness
- Grace in hard times
- Grace in growth
- Grace in deadlines

- Grace in service
- Grace in judgments
- Grace in love
- Grace in rootedness
- Grace in authenticity
- Grace in absolutes
- Grace in endurance
- Grace in extending grace

Grace is our 24/7 ministry leadership obligation because that is the commitment to grace Christ Jesus made to us.

Grace at Work

As believers, we are thankful for the transforming power of the grace we've received in Christ. We are committed to passing on grace, just as Jesus instructed His disciples, "Give as freely as you have received!" (Matt. 10:8).

Unfortunately, I see too many leaders purposefully switch off grace the moment they show up to work—even in Christian ministries. Instead of open arms of grace, their folded arms support a boss "game-day face" that is tough, demanding, harsh, and gives no quarter. And this often happens while they have a Bible sitting open on the corner of their desk.

Why? It's because poor leadership modeling and teaching of the past has taught us that a spirit of grace will undermine our commitment to success, quality, productivity, efficiency, and accountability. We have had it drilled into us that if we are soft or satisfied with less than excellence, the effectiveness of the entire team will suffer. This is old-school nonsense!

Would Jesus call us to a leadership responsibility, and then ask us to set aside the cornerstone of the Christian life because it is time to go to work? Of course not. It is time to ignore the world's pattern, and allow grace to become the hallmark of your leadership.

Part 4

PREPARE TO BE SHOCKED

Are you ready for God to bring opportunities? Doing so will require you to leave what is secure. The journey may be scary, you'll feel out of control, and most importantly, you will be required to get going without knowing exactly where you are headed.

Sound familiar? That was the journey of Abraham, who by faith "obeyed when God called him to leave home and go to another land that God would give him as his inheritance. He went without knowing where he was going" (Heb. 11:8).

You probably have much in common with Abraham:

- He was an established leader. Abraham was old when God called him and had every excuse for staying with his plan rather than chasing something new.

- He was comfortable. Abraham lived in Mesopotamia, home of the world's first civilization, and God was asking him to head into the wilderness.

- He was rooted. Abraham had a massive operation, and it was all working well, so he didn't want to risk the future by changing everything.

You and Abraham share another commonality: a desire to be obedient to God's leading. In capturing God-inspired opportunities, we achieve kingdom purposes.

It is not recorded if Abraham prayed for this opportunity. Most likely not, because the toughness of God's demands was shocking. "Leave your native country, your relatives, and your father's family, and go to the land that I will show you" (Gen. 12:1).

At the same time, the enormity of God's promises was even more shocking. "I will make you into a great nation. I will bless you and make you famous, and you will be a blessing to others. I will bless those who bless you and curse those who treat you with contempt. All the families on earth will be blessed through you" (Gen. 12:2–3).

Are you ready to pray for opportunities? God will bring them if you're willing to respond. And, if so, prepare to be shocked.

Chapter 18

I Never Planned . . .

I never planned . . . to give up planning.

A brief transparent sidebar comment completely changed my perspective about leadership. I don't think the sage meant to say it, and when he blurted it out, it was a bit awkward considering who he was, who he represented, and who was in the room.

It happened like this—

Having arrived as a new college president, I had inherited a boat-load of problems that put our accreditation at risk. Accreditors carry enormous power over colleges and universities. They demand academic integrity, fiscal stability, systematic controls, and procedures for multi-layered comprehensive planning. Coming up short in any of their standards could trigger significant complications or even lead to closure.

These agencies are run by professional staff, but peer university presidents and academic leaders set the benchmark standards. They make the decisions too. Thus, every institution has a stake in each institution's accreditation standing because their reputations are intertwined through this shared governance structure.

My college's difficulties were numerous, but the most complex was meeting the accreditor's expectation to put in place a robust planning cycle that links goals to plans to expenditures to results to evaluation and then circles back to a new set of goals. The guidance regulations were vague, but the threats requiring upgrading our planning mechanism were concrete. This challenge came before I had personally moved away from planning, so I was all for establishing the planning system. I just didn't know what mechanism would be approved.

I'm amazed at how many CEOs won't ask for help when they are stuck. I'm not in that category. Facing this grave challenge, I wanted to find the best help possible and called a fellow university president, Tom Corts. He was president of Samford University and also chaired the accrediting board. He guided the establishment of the required planning benchmarks, and thus, was the ultimate authority.

He graciously volunteered to come to our campus. I was thrilled to have the most experienced Christian university president in the country, who was also the ultimate authority for the accrediting body, headed my way—and he was bringing with him his vice president for planning. In just a day, with their expertise, we created a planning model that worked for our institution and the accreditor.

But my take-away from that consultation was not passing an evaluation hurdle. Instead, after reviewing the vice president's planning structure, Tom offered, what was for me, a life-changing insight. Reflecting on what we were about to undertake, Tom summarized our newly christened planning system, saying:

> You will need this process for the accreditors, but when I look back at my career as president, our most significant advances never came out of our planning. God brought the big things through unexpected opportunities.[1]

That moment shook my approach to leadership. The seeds of Opportunity Leadership were planted deeply, even as Tom's vice president for planning assured me how important planning would be to our future.

Since that day many years ago, I've discovered that almost every Christian leader feels the same about planning when they reflect on how God has guided their path. Most continue to be engaged in a formal planning process but are also quick to acknowledge that their life's pivotal events were rarely planned.

Leith Anderson, former mega-church pastor and NAE president, captured well this tug between the two models when he said, "I think I have the planning gene. But I learned to love the surprises of God that have repeatedly exceeded my plans." That is a good place to be as a ministry leader.

> I NEVER PLANNED . . . TO GIVE UP PLANNING.

Through these pages, I have shared my personal stories demonstrating how Opportunity Leadership works in real time. However, these types of experiences are not unique to me. Treasuring opportunities is nearly universal across the entire spectrum of Christian leaders. Being shaped by opportunities is their common thread, whether it influences calling, new initiatives, career change, platform of influence, or even being fired. The commonality of their stories is delighting in God's opportunities.

It is inspiring to learn from what they never planned.

I Never Planned This Future . . .

- "Faith requires moving into a risk zone that only God can fill. It moves us from being in full control, so plans are met only as He enables. There really is no Plan B." —Brian Stiller

- "An author wrote that pastors should give a vision speech of plans for the future. I worked hard on my speech and was uncomfortable that my predictions were so outrageously ambitious. It didn't take long for me to quit giving vision speeches because God's actual blessings made my visions seem silly and small." —Leith Anderson

- "For eight months, I awoke each morning feeling nauseous and questioning my judgment. Then I concluded that God surely had a plan." —Kirk D. Farney

- "To act boldly, we must also take time to listen deeply." —Leighton Ford

I Never Planned This Calling . . .

- "I never planned it, but looking back, God had His fingerprints all over my life in providing me leadership opportunities in preparation." —David Brickner

- "My 'yes' when I wanted it to be 'no' changed the direction of my life." —Jerry White

- "I didn't chart it out on a whiteboard. It wasn't even my initial career path. It was an opportunity I simply couldn't ignore. No grand scheme made it happen. Opportunity opened the way, and positive results fueled my passion." —Les Parrott

- "I have learned, when Divine Providence calls, I answer the phone." —Al Lopus

- "My high school dis-appointment had translated into His-appointment for my life." —Doug Birdsall

I Never Planned This Path . . .

- "God has faithfully brought me from one mountain to a different mountain, but I learn more about Him and myself in the valleys than on the mountain tops." —Bob Doll

- "Following one goal of preaching the gospel, and obeying His call one step at a time. The contours of my ministry path were orchestrated by God." —Billy Kim

Their stories, and those of others, may trigger insights for a future you never planned. Dream a bit and see where it takes you. Or, as better said by my friend Carmen LaBerge, "I never planned to write this for Roger's book. You likely never planned to read this. But here we are. Isn't God great? Where else would we have met and had the opportunity to share and reflect and dream and grow together?"

Unplanned Provision

Steve Moore, who served for decades as CEO of the M.J. Murdock Charitable Trust, succinctly puts into perspective the providence of opportunities. He never planned:

> . . . to be surprised by God. In fact, I realize now how many of the surprises were at first misunderstood. As I came to understand and believe that God is much too good to be cruel and much too wise to make a mistake, I began to recognize God at work in the world and my life in more ways than I ever was fully aware. What a surprise!
>
> A phone call I first thought to be an interruption became a providential moment. An argument with a friend became a breakthrough moment to greater intimacy. A dream dashed opened the way for a heart-filling vision. An inconvenient, annoying trip paved the way for a conversation of eternal significance with a loved one. A small expression of encouragement became a God-shaped infusion of hope.
>
> His ways are often not my ways. In the kingdom economy, He is always at work, and nothing is wasted. What a surprise! Why was that so hard to see? Now I'll plan for more surprises, or at least, hopefully, be more ready to recognize them when they come.

Unplanned Salvation

The opportunity to grow up in a stable Christian home is a gift too many leaders take for granted. It may be the most important opportunity God has ever given you. But others took an astonishing route into the arms of Christ. One of those is a pioneer in biblical reconciliation—a champion—Dr. John Perkins:

> I grew up in a sharecroppers shack on a plantation in Mississippi, was nearly beaten to death in a county jail for protesting segregation, and my life was filled with rage learning my brother was unjustly shot to death by a policeman. With such a beginning, I never could have imagined God was preparing me to become a Bible teacher and spend sixty-three years learning and telling the story of the gospel.
>
> My three-year-old son lead me to Christ. When I was twenty-seven years old, he went to a Good News Club, and he learned a song I'd never heard before: *Jesus loves the little children. All the children of the world. Red, brown, yellow, black, and white. They are precious in His sight. Jesus loves the little children of the world.*
>
> That was the first time I heard the central message of the gospel: God loves little children. I did not come to God believing there were black Christians and white Christians and red, yellow, and brown Christians. I heard the central message of why He came to the world. My son taught me the centrality of the gospel.
>
> This inspiration got me thinking about God. The more I thought about God, the more I wanted to learn, so I went to a Bible bookstore I'd heard about. At that time, I didn't even know there were Christian bookstores. The one near me in Monrovia, California, was owned by Mary Feaster.

I Never Planned . . .

I found out later Mary had been a missionary in Brazil, so having served in a multi-cultural environment, she warmly welcomed a young black man into her store that day in 1957.

I told her, "I want to buy a Bible because I want to become a Bible teacher." She said, "Wonderful. You know the Bible is about one central person and others that work together with Him to tell the story about Him. But it is all one story." She said, "You have to know the whole Bible and read the whole Bible." So I started reading and came to the story about Abraham: God said, "I will make your name great and give you gifts, and you will be blessed."

For a sharecropper's son with a third-grade education, the Lord has blessed me with opportunities to share the gospel far beyond what anyone would have ever dreamed possible.

Unplanned Calling

A variety of leaders point to an unexpected opportunity as direction-setting for their calling. For some, this came early, and for others, it was a mid-career change.

Doug Birdsall, Honorary Chair of the Lausanne Movement, shares how his disappointment as a high school football player proved to be part of God's preparation for a calling he could not have anticipated. Doug was the starting fullback, ready to take the spotlight in his high school senior year. But a more talented junior emerged, leaving Doug with the choice of either giving up his love for football or becoming a "lowly guard" on the offensive line:

> A switch flipped on in my mind. I *was* no longer a fullback. I now *am* a guard! I determined to "give it all I've got." A guard's job is to protect the star players. A guard finds his greatest satisfaction in helping the team accomplish more together

227

than what even the greatest athletes could do on their own. Playing guard became a metaphor for my life's work. For twenty years, I was a missionary in the group-oriented society of Japan. My job was to help Japanese pastors fulfill their vision and enable younger missionaries to discover and fulfill their most significant giftedness areas. During the following ten years, I was involved in providing leadership for the Lausanne Movement, helping it pursue its mission: "the Whole Church taking the Whole Gospel to the Whole World."

During the Lausanne Congress opening celebration in Cape Town, South Africa, I looked out over those leaders from 198 countries, and a surprising thought came to my mind. "I am not the most gifted leader, the most brilliant scholar, or the most eloquent speaker here. I'm a guard!" My assignment was to help create an environment in which 4,200 "star players"—established and emerging leaders—could learn, connect, and strategize on behalf of the global church.

For forty years, I had been learning to block. My high school dis-appointment had translated into His-appointment for my life.

Lots of leaders identify with Doug's experience. The calling we envision takes shape much differently as God directs us by opening and closing doors.

> THE CALLING WE ENVISION TAKES SHAPE MUCH DIFFERENTLY AS GOD DIRECTS US BY OPENING AND CLOSING DOORS.

My younger brother, Les Parrott, is a *New York Times* best-selling author of *Saving Your Marriage Before It Starts* and the founder of SYMBIS.com. Les is well known as a marriage and family author. Most who have read his books don't know that this is not what he set out to do:

I never planned to devote my life's work to helping couples figure out the ins and outs of marriage. My wife, Leslie, and I never had pre-marriage counseling, but we spent the first year of our marriage in therapy. It's the truth. We married within a week after graduating from college and then moved from Chicago to Los Angeles for graduate school. That first year was tough.

We soon learned that lots of young couples were headed toward marriage with little preparation. So, we launched a weekend event for students interested in marriage and eventually wrote a book from what we learned. Not long after, our ideas were featured in a *USA Today* story, and soon we found ourselves on the national stage to talk about marriage.

It wasn't my original plan. It was a glaring need and an opportunity to meet it. I didn't chart it out on a whiteboard. It wasn't even my initial career path. It was an opportunity I simply couldn't ignore. No grand scheme made it happen; opportunity opened the way, and positive results fueled my passion.

An unshakable commitment to a calling must be grounded in absolute assurance the new direction is God-inspired. Christian statesman Leighton Ford lived out his axiom that "to act boldly, we must also take time to listen deeply." Describing a crucial international meeting he was chairing, Leighton abruptly stopped a discussion escalating into division and called for an hour of prayer. It was during that pause that he caught a vision for something he had never planned that dramatically shifted his personal ministry focus from big-arena evangelism to mentoring:

During that hour, a young leader from England, in his prayer, quoted Isaiah 43:18–19, "Forget the former things;

do not dwell on the past. See, I am doing a new thing! Now it springs up, do you not perceive it?" (NIV). Those words went like an arrow to my heart. My wife Jeanie and I had been sensing the need to identify and develop young leaders emerging around the world. We had prayed for a word from Scripture to confirm that call.

Those words were the confirmation. Thirty years of preaching the gospel around the world had been fruitful and fulfilling. Now there was something new!

For others, God surprises them by sending ambassadors with the message. Kirk Farney, Vice President for Advancement, Vocation, and Alumni Engagement at Wheaton College, was trapped in a choice between his lucrative established career in international banking or his unquenched passion for studying church history:

While going through this season of soul-searching, God independently sent two different trusted coworkers to see me with challenging insight within a matter of hours. Each expressed concern for my well-being, noting that my normally upbeat personality had disappeared. They told me to take care of myself, even if it meant stepping away from banking, and "turn it all over to God."

In between these conversations, a partner at a major law firm called me out of the blue. He said that I was on his mind inexplicably that morning, then added, "I don't know how things are going for you right now, but it occurs to me that you should consider pursuing your love of learning and go back to grad school." Suddenly, the idea of stepping away from banking to pursue a PhD in religious history went from a fanciful pipe dream to a genuine possibility.

Other leaders, too, sensed God's call to a new path, even though they were unsure of the next steps. Kathy Thibodeaux was the principal dancer for a major ballet company. After finding Christ, she longed to use her gifts more explicitly for God's work by forming a ballet company committed to the ministry of dance. With no plan, no dancers, and not even a rehearsal studio, she gave up a top position in the world of dance for an unknown future:

> Because I was well known in the area, a local radio station interviewed me about this dramatic change, and for the first time publicly, I articulated what God was calling me to do—but didn't have a plan for how it was to come about. But I believed God had given me this gift of dance and that He had a purpose for it. Astonishingly, a near-by college president heard my interview while driving to work and called to offer free studio space on his campus.
>
> With that start, Ballet Magnificat! was born—the world's first professional Christian dance company. Through the years, we've performed across the globe, trained thousands of dancers, and even helped our first sponsor, Belhaven University, develop the world's premier Christian collegiate dance program.

Some leaders have had their "half-time" calling reset while headed toward early retirement. Al Lopus recounts how an unexpected phone call asked him to help a project *Christianity Today* was considering to create a list of the best Christian places to work. Al was finishing up a successful career as a pioneer in surveying corporate employment satisfaction:

> From business experience, I developed a heartfelt belief that Christian teams and organizations should set the standard as

the most effective places to work in the world. After eighteen years, The Best Christian Workplaces Institute has served over 1,000 churches, Christian non-profits, and Christian-led businesses. We equip and inspire Christian leaders to create a flourishing workplace.

Faithfully, we have followed the opportunities God has provided. I have learned, when Divine Providence calls, I answer the phone.

Obstructions Become Opportunities

I enjoy reading biographies of historical figures, not to remember their well-known accomplishments, but to understand the struggles they overcame to achieve outcomes on which legacies are built. As leaders, we tend to look at our contemporary peers and assume their path to significance was well-plotted along a steady line of success. On the contrary, every public leader has lived out a story of pushing through the overwhelming challenges before achieving results admired by others.

Ron Blue is well known as an enormously successful and influential financial guru. Still, his path included a fork in the road that demanded courage and tenacity to find his eventual calling. After he and his wife became Christians, he left his successful finance career to join Cru in full-time ministry. That was the plan, but God had a direction Ron hadn't planned:

> I had just finished my tenth trip to Africa over two years, working on an evangelistic campaign there. On weekends I was teaching leadership seminars so that I was gone from home 60 to 70 percent of the time, leaving a wife with five children under the age of eleven with no support from friends, family, or me.

She called me at the office one day after about two years and said, "How do you get unChristianed?" Of course, I was stunned and said, "What do you mean?" And she said, "If this is the abundant life, I've had all the abundance I can take."

That led us to spend an evening thinking through our real goals, values, and priorities and decided to get back into financial work. But this time, only working with Christians and helping them make financial decisions based upon a biblical worldview of life.

I was headed in one direction, but God had a different direction. Long story short, forty years later, that firm serves over 10,000 clients collectively, giving over $150 million per year, and manages $11 billion.

A vast array of leaders found a new calling because they ran up against an overwhelming roadblock. Liza Looser, founder of the Cirlot Agency, built from scratch one of the top marketing and public relations firms serving the banking industry. Then, in the 1990s, when banking regulations dramatically shifted, that portion of her business went from 75 percent to 5 percent of revenue within only twelve months:

> We knew we had to pivot, and we had to do it in a hurry. The answer came from an unexpected source—a long-time friendship with Ingalls Shipbuilding. For their sixtieth anniversary, they asked us to capture the heartfelt stories of the heroes whose names appear on Ingalls-built ships. It was a fascinating project but in an industry far outside our normal strike-zone of expertise.
>
> Through our work, they won an enormous military contract. On that success, we shifted all of our new business efforts to the aerospace/defense industry. The great news: companies started calling! Looking back over the years, it

has been my privilege to become business partners, but most importantly, friends with people who have dedicated their lives to their God-given calling of changing this world for the better and keeping America and our allies safe.

Many leaders found their dream job when their dream job was out of reach. Mary Landron Darden, the founder of Higher Education Innovation, was on a well-planned career path to a college presidency. She had taken every essential preparatory step. All the boxes were checked. Although an excellent candidate, she was always nudged out by someone else because God had something only she could do:

> My higher education leadership focus had always been exploring, working, and developing new higher education models, looking toward the future and what was most important about moving successfully into that future. Maybe this career roadblock was God directing me to help leaders research and train for college administration innovation—to give them the data and ideas that the job's daily grind doesn't allow them to envision.
>
> Today I help leaders and institutions to undergo the significant, necessary, and bold metamorphosis into how to serve this radically changing new world. The paycheck was not impressive, but the joy is there. In this role, I can do the blue-sky dreaming about higher education that would have been impossible as a sitting institutional president.

Unintended Influence

In hearing their stories, I've found that most leaders who are well-known through books, media, or conference keynotes did not plan their path. God elevated them out of humble beginnings to a place of public responsibility. The most remarkable of all is Billy Kim, whose journey I recounted in the last chapter. What God had planned was far beyond anything Sgt. Carl Powers, Billy Kim, or anyone else could imagine.

I never planned to interpret for the audacious '73 Billy Graham Crusade in Seoul, Korea, attended by 1.1 million people in the final meeting. This event then brought the mega-church movement to South Korea, and now South Korea sends the largest number of missionaries worldwide next to the USA.

I never imagined I would serve as the senior pastor of Suwon Central Baptist Church for over forty-five years or be the first non-Westerner elected president of the Baptist World Alliance. I never planned to have the privilege of spreading the Good News of the gospel through leading the FEBC-Korea radio ministry or bringing my heartfelt funeral eulogy for a good friend, Rev. Billy Graham.

Our Sovereign God laid out these pathways, and my role was simply to stay the course, following one goal of preaching the gospel and obeying His call one step at a time.

Steve Douglass, president emeritus of Cru, the largest Christian ministry in the world, also never planned a path of leadership but was simply being faithful to his call to share the gospel with as many people as he could reach:

In the late 1970s, I was feeling frustrated about not having meaningful opportunities to do evangelism. So, I started praying that God would open a door for me. What happened after that was a succession of events I didn't plan but turned out to be God's very fruitful opportunities.

Shortly after praying, I started getting invitations to speak to Christian Women's Club "men's night" events. These were occasions where Christian women could invite their husbands to hear a presentation of the gospel. I developed a talk on personal development, where I shared my testimony for about twenty minutes, transitioned to a presentation of the gospel, and closed with an opportunity for people to ask Christ into their lives.

But what happened next was even more amazing! I decided to try the same seminar approach but in a campus setting. The topic wasn't personal development. It was, "How to Get Better Grades and Have More Fun." I taught a few big ideas on how to do better as a student, shared my testimony, presented the gospel, and gave an opportunity to respond. I spoke on the "grades" topic about 300 times. Thousands of students indicated decisions for Christ as a result.

Now, think back with me what God used to make that happen: I was frustrated because I couldn't do evangelism well enough. I prayed that God would intervene, and He supernaturally opened doors that led me to evangelistic opportunities and effectiveness beyond what I could have planned or imagined possible.

Carmen LaBerge, author and radio talk show host, never planned a path that would lead her to spend every weekday morning with thousands of people:

I anticipate miracles, offer myself as a ready instrument for God's use, and—to the very best of my ability—do the next right thing that aligns with my gifting and mission. Along the way, that has meant I have served in congregation ministry, national ministry, ecumenical ministry, and now on the faculty of a university with a media ministry where I teach thousands of people every day via live radio. I never planned any of it.

How does all that happen? Moment by moment. Day by day. Week by week. Month by month. Year by year. Decade by decade. For a lifetime, that, when looking back, reveals a strategic plan that I experienced as one grace-filled opportunity after another.

The co-founder of Truth at Work, Ray Hilbert, also never sought a platform of influence. In response to a friend who wouldn't let go of a book idea, God gave to Ray what he could never have planned:

> *The Janitor: How an Unexpected Friendship Transformed a CEO and His Company* was birthed. And, in my wildest dreams, I would never have anticipated it would strike such a chord to be read all over the world by nearly two million people. That, you just can't plan.

Not seeking the responsibility, African enterprise leader Michael Cassidy found himself unexpectedly thrust into an entirely new arena of influence in the tension of South Africa's effort to confront apartheid:

> As tensions enormously escalated, the idea occurred to us to take teams of pan-African political leaders around South Africa to meet and pray with the various political parties' leaders, from far left to far right. It was an amazing time, and we found that many of these leaders were talking similar language about racial peace and national prosperity. While they spoke to us about this, they never spoke to each other about it.

Long story short, despairing of their efforts to create a peaceful environment for the upcoming elections, De Klerk, Mandela, and Buthelezi decided to call in a group of international peacemakers led by Henry Kissinger and Lord Carrington, former British foreign secretary. The conference broke down after twenty-four hours, with everyone going home and Kissinger predicting Armageddon soon for South Africa. An informal message from the US State Department indicated they expected a million dead in the next two weeks.

With time running out fast and only a couple of weeks before the 1994 elections, we insisted others in South Africa keep meeting. The miraculous outcome was a document, produced by Washington Okumu, our man in the equation, which allowed the parties to go forward peacefully into these history-making elections and a new day for South Africa.

A leader's influence is not measured simply by what they directly touch but also what they pass on to others. Michael Moe, founder of Global Silicon Valley and author of *Finding the Next Starbucks,* invests in start-up companies but didn't have a plan for investing in the next generation of entrepreneurs:

I've had a prayer for many years to use my gifts and platform to help more people participate in the future. As an investor and passionate advocate for education technology, I hoped to back someone who had a scalable solution for offering "Weapons of Mass Instruction" for rising entrepreneurs. Entrepreneurs solve problems. They fix things.

I was hoping for someone to come along and request investment capital for that kind of educational start-up, when my friend Michael Clifford asked me how I was going to use my experience to have the greatest impact. Old MacDonald

had a farm . . . EIEIO. New MacDonald has a startup . . .
EIEIO . . . it's about Entrepreneurship, Innovation, Education, Impact, and Opportunity.

Why wouldn't I create an online MBA for entrepreneurs?
He had the perfect partner for me to do this: Belhaven University in Jackson, Mississippi. The next thing I knew, I was
on the phone with Dr. Roger Parrott, and several weeks later,
I was on campus mapping out how we were going to execute
this program. I pray my legacy will be in giving others the
tools to be equipped for discovering God's opportunities for
their future.

Capturing Opportunities

Trusting God for opportunities that take us far beyond our best plans
is inspiring. One of the best stories capturing this trusting outlook
comes from Leith Anderson, president emeritus of the National Association of Evangelicals and pastor emeritus of one of the most
influential churches in the world:

> The old church building was on nine-tenths of an acre with
> fourteen parking places. Lots of stairs kept away anyone in
> a wheelchair with physical limitations or handicaps. It was
> big enough to keep in current parishioners and small enough
> to keep out newcomers. So we decided to relocate on an
> 82-percent congregational vote. But, some of the 18 percent
> were vocally and persuasively opposed.
>
> The risky choice was to buy thirty-one acres three towns
> and nine miles away. The old church building didn't have a
> high market value, and buying land and constructing a new
> building required scary loans. The new building was smaller
> than the old but had more parking. Critics told me I was a

bad pastor and leader who would destroy the church. They said no one would come and that a majority of the congregation would stay with the building since it was purchased by a megachurch starting a third campus.

Dream or plan? I'm not sure it was that I hoped to someday be the pastor of a church with 1,000 in attendance. Probably not likely. I sort of planned just in case the unlikely dream might come true.

The first Sunday in the new facility was in July, and my nightmare was that no one would come. I planned for few to shield myself from disappointment. To my great surprise, God showed up with 1,500 worshippers. I was flabbergasted. But, pessimistic planning told me this was a one-off opening day never to be repeated. In the middle of a hot Minnesota summer, they kept coming every weekend, and our plans required three morning services and then four morning services, and eventually seven weekend services.

Wooddale Church in Eden Prairie became a large congregation of thousands (although we never posted or announced the numbers). Generosity led to becoming one of the top ten missions-giving churches in the country. People came from every strata of the area—unemployed job seekers who were helped so much that the *New York Times* wrote about it; office holders from the local school board to the legislature to the governor's mansion; anchors from all the network television stations; CEOs from major corporations. Newcomers. New believers. Nine daughter churches were started by recruiting people to leave the mother church by the hundreds that multiplied into thousands—far more attending the daughter churches than on the mother church campus.

An author wrote that pastors should give a vision speech of plans for the future. I worked hard on my speech and was uncomfortable that my predictions were so outrageously ambitious. It didn't take long for me to quit giving vision speeches because God's actual blessings made my visions seem silly and small.

Whether, responding to a career-long calling or short-term crisis, the characteristics of trusting God for opportunities are similar. As COVID-19 gripped the nation, Tom Phillips and the Billy Graham Evangelistic Association transformed their small phone center overnight:

People were hurting, desiring hope, and full of fear because of the coronavirus pandemic. There was no vaccine. We were set up to receive only fifty calls simultaneously, but we trusted God to turn a pandemic of fear into a pandemic of faith. Within days we invested in equipment and recruited a team to handle lots more phone calls. Within three minutes after the first Fox News ad ran late one night, 660 calls were received. It was an amazing response. Our teams were virtually overwhelmed. People would call over and over until they got through to us, calling back twenty or thirty times if necessary.

All the years of preparation in our discipleship training team, sixty or more years, came to fruition. Who would have dreamed that in only nine months we would see over 300,000 actual callers prayed with, over 18,000 decisions for Christ, and nearly 9,000 first-time salvation decisions.

Looking to my familiar Christian higher education world, there are endless new ventures that would have been impossible if God hadn't brought an opportunity. At Houghton College, president Shirley Mullen recounts how a friendship launched their cutting-edge data science degree:

It all came about in the context of reaching out to one of our alumni to join the President's Advisory Board. She told me what she was doing and how her Houghton education in the liberal arts had prepared her to be a pioneer in the emerging field of data science. Teaming with our remarkable faculty, her large and fearless imagination inspired the creation of the academic major, a national network of alumni in the field, [and] a stream of graduates establishing a reputation for excellence.

Kim Phipps, president of Messiah University, recounts how they didn't have the bandwidth or budget to tackle another large-scale project after the 2008 recession, let alone one that would require costly specialized space and equipment:

Then, a community leader contacted us with an unbelievable offer: a technical school had vacated a large space in an ideally located office building. We could complete their lease (eighteen months at no cost to us!) and begin transforming the space into the classrooms and dedicated labs we needed to dramatically expand our graduate programs.

President Phil Ryken of Wheaton College never planned to transform a fifty-year-old science building into a "state-of-the-art conservatory complex that would touch the music-loving soul of every student on campus and become what one guest performer called a new Chicagoland jewel":

It was time for old Armerding Hall to be torn down—that was the conventional thinking. Although the building had served Wheaton College well for half a century, it needed to give way to the larger, more contemporary facilities that our exceptional music program desperately needed.

So, we decided to build a new conservatory that would provide the quality music facilities needed to fulfill our mission. As we shared our plans with prospective donors—complete with a three-dimensional model—we found them decidedly uninspired by the design to the degree that it would jeopardize our fundraising efforts. After all, it takes more than a set of drawings to complete a building; it also takes money.

We decided to take a second look at renovating Armerding Hall. This time the constraints started to look more like opportunities as both the architects and musicians stretched their creativity. Today, the Armerding Center for Music and the Arts stands as a visible testimony to the truth of Proverbs 16:9: "The heart of man plans his way, but the LORD establishes his steps" (ESV).

Tyndale University's former president, Brian Stiller, may have had the boldest opportunity of all, coming in to rescue an institution nearly bankrupt, and then moving the entire campus:

In my second year, we were hanging on by our fiscal fingernails. On a September Sunday afternoon, as we were about to turn into the road leading to the college, we passed a fifty-six-acre campus owned by the Sisters of St. Joseph. My wife Lily turned to me, quietly pointed to the campus, and said, "Brian, someday the Lord will give that to you." That became a defining opportunity, an idea that nurtured determination in the team to solve the immediate problems to be ready to capture what we saw lying ahead. Today Tyndale University, including a first-class seminary, enjoys that beautiful campus and is alive and well because a seeming tragedy became an opportunity.

The lesson of this experience—building out of thirty-five years of ministry—was this: faith is exercised by the will. It requires moving into a risk zone where what we attempt is beyond our capacity to fulfill. Risk is that space that only God can fill. It moves us from being in full control, so plans are met only as He enables. There really is no Plan B.

Unexpected Leadership

Examining the stories of ministry leadership, many came to it not seeking the role. David Brickner planned to be a professional musician, but God was preparing him to become the leader of Jews for Jesus:

> I never planned it, but looking back, God had His fingerprints all over my life in providing me leadership opportunities in preparation. Early on, I was thrust into leadership, often in very challenging environments. Each successive leadership opportunity had me initially feeling completely inadequate, but each time I have found God's grace sufficient for the task. Looking back, each of these opportunities was building up a diversity of valuable leadership skills. But none of it was planned. It was a God-orchestrated life-long journey of "scaling up" in leadership.

When first elected president of the Navigators, Jerry White tried to avoid a prestigious leadership opportunity, but God knew what was best. Obedience to opportunity reshaped his framework for leading that great international ministry:

> I never planned to become an Air Force general. As a leader in The Navigators, I was already sensitive that our international staff would not understand my long military background and

involvement in our nation's space efforts. After all, in many nations, the military is feared rather than respected. Yet God had led me to stay in the Air Force Reserves when coming with The Navigators after thirteen and a half years of active duty. Shortly after being selected to become international president, I planned to retire from the Air Force as a colonel.

I was serving my last active duty tour in a very classified assignment when I received a call from a long-time friend and major general. He asked me to stay active and take an assignment as my commander's reserve assistant, which was a brigadier general's position. I said, "Tom, I really can't do that. I have just taken the responsibility to lead The Navigators, so I simply would not have the time."

Our outgoing president, Lorne Sanny, listened thoughtfully but didn't respond while relaying my decision to turn down the military promotion and leadership opportunity. The next morning Lorne came into my office and simply said, "Jerry, don't turn that down so quickly because you don't know what God might have in store." That was not what I wanted to hear. I feared how it would look to our international staff. I feared the time it would take. I feared that it might affect my ability to lead The Navigators. Mary and I prayed about it again.

Long story short, I took the assignment and was promoted after a year to brigadier general. I was stretched beyond measure. But that experience was invaluable in learning to lead a large organization like The Navigators.

Four years after becoming president and being promoted to general, our only son was brutally murdered. That impacted not only Mary, me, and our family, but our entire Navigator family and my Air Force relationships. We became broken. We became vulnerable. People gathered around us—believers and non-believers alike. I had not planned it, but God orchestrated all of it for the good of the kingdom. It impacted The Navigators in transformational ways.

My "yes" when I wanted it to be "no" changed the direction of my life.

Through a very different set of circumstances, Paul Cedar had no intention of making a change while serving as senior pastor of a large, historic church in Southern California that was in the midst of a massive building project:

One evening, I received an unexpected call from the chairman of a denominational committee searching for a new president. I thanked him for his call but explained that I could not consider a change in position at that time. Also, I was not interested in serving as a denominational president. I thought that was the end of the conversation, but they kept contacting me.

Much to our surprise, after much prayer and fasting, a year later, my wife Jeanie and I both reached the conclusion that our Lord wanted us to go in obedience to Him. That led us to many years of fruitful ministry with the denomination. At the same time, the Lord continued to bless the church and the flock that we left behind and loved so deeply.

Being sought for a job is one thing, but being fired is completely different. But even in that, God brings opportunity. Painfully, sometimes, the only way God can get us to consider a change is to give us a hard jolt. Bob Doll was the last person you'd ever expect to be fired, with his enormous following as a regular guest on CNBC and other market-watch television programs, speaking as the chief strategist for the largest investment firm in the world:

I never planned to leave my job in 2012. I was fired instead. Not seeing this coming, it hit me hard as I had unknowingly transferred my identity to my work. I felt lost. Who am I without this job? Perhaps for the first time in my adult life, I had to relinquish control—a difficult but necessary spiritual lesson, especially for a Type A male.

Work/career/positions had all become an idol. Being productive and doing had unknowingly become an attempt at self-redemption. Ever so slowly, I came to realize that trusting anything to deliver the security, significance, and satisfaction that only the one true God can give is a dead-end alley. The time between jobs gave me a real but gut-wrenching opportunity to deal with clarification of God's calling in my life and to sense the rich fellowship in prayer and in presence with the body of Christ.

While I never want to repeat being fired, at the same time, I wouldn't trade the lessons learned for anything. God has faithfully brought me from one mountain to a different mountain, but I learn more about Him and myself in the valleys than on the mountain tops.

Your Story: "Wow"

Looking ahead at the sweeping survey of challenges in your ministry's future, you could easily become overwhelmed. The path is unclear, the obstacles appear enormous, and the options seem few. Looking forward, you may be prone to throw up your hands and say, "Yikes!"

Instead, take your eyes off the future and turn around to look backward. Reflect on how many times God has safely brought you and other leaders through a maze of obstacles. From this vantage point, trace in detail how the Lord intervened—getting you around, over, or through every challenge. Your path is crystal clear in hindsight.

PREPARE TO BE SHOCKED BY THE WONDER AND AWE OF GOD'S UNWAVERING PROVISION.

If you will examine closely where you've been, you'll realize your past trials look much like your problems that appear overwhelming in the future. From this perspective, looking back to gain confidence for how God will lead you ahead, the only response is, "Wow!"

Like all these leaders' stories, yours, too, will be a story of an overwhelming challenge being transformed into a surprising opportunity you never planned. Prepare to be shocked by the wonder and awe of God's unwavering provision.

Epilogue

Opportunity Leadership in Action

G oliath never had a chance!

David's three oldest brothers were with King Saul and the Israelite army preparing to fight the Philistines, while David took care of the chores at home. As he was tending his father's sheep, he also developed skill with the most potent weapon a shepherd can use to protect vulnerable flocks from lions and bears: his sling.

When David's father asked him to take food to his brothers and their army commanders, he didn't go with a plan to fight Goliath. It was a God-chosen Opportunity Leadership moment—a challenge that directed the rest of his life and the nation of Israel for generations to come.

> GOLIATH NEVER HAD A CHANCE BECAUSE GOD WAS ON DAVID'S SIDE.

In many ways, this well-known story reflects the bedrock principles of Opportunity Leadership:

- David acted fast. He didn't hesitate to step forward while everyone else was frozen in fear. The two armies had been facing each other for over a month, with neither willing to make a move. Opportunity Leaders are comfortable with risk and know that speed matters.

- David capitalized on his unique strengths and resisted the temptation to follow the patterns of others. Not caving to the power differential, David knew his gifts and refused to exchange his expertise with a sling for the protection of King Saul's armor. Opportunity Leaders know their strengths and rely upon them to fulfill their mission.

- David knew he would win, but he didn't expect to accomplish his goal on the first attempt. David took five stones to fight one giant because experience taught that first attempts are rarely fully successful. Opportunity Leaders flex during implementation and stay nimble enough to change and adjust in mid-course.

- David was supported by others, but ultimately stood alone. He walked unaccompanied into the valley to face Goliath and was on full display for both his advocates and adversaries to watch his success or failure. Opportunity Leaders get out front to lead.

- David approached the opportunity with confidence. David trusted God: "The LORD who rescued me from the claws of the lion and the bear will rescue me from this Philistine!" (1 Sam. 17:37). Although Goliath scared the entire Israelite army, a lumbering giant wearing one hundred pounds of armor may have looked to David like an easy opponent compared to past antagonists. Opportunity Leaders trust God to bring the right opportunities.

The eventful day that David and his sling conquered the giant may be the most-often-referenced Bible story. From business to sports, the phrase "David and Goliath" has become a metaphor to describe improbable successes. The message of this epic encounter is, as everyone tells it, underdogs can be victorious over the powerful.

But that is not the point of the story! The takeaway from this great saga is that Goliath never had a chance because God was on David's side.

This battle was the Lord's, not David's. And when our opportunities appear to be blocked by giants, we can, like David, run toward our challenge with confidence, knowing God is on our side (1 Sam. 17:48).

> GOD IS MORE
> POWERFUL THAN
> OUR MINDS COULD
> EVER COMPREHEND—
> BUT WE DON'T LEAD
> LIKE HE IS.

Reflecting on his life, David implores us to understand the enormity of God's power as we face overwhelming challenges: "The LORD is my rock, my fortress, and my savior; my God is my rock, in whom I find protection" (Ps. 18:2).

God is more powerful than our minds could ever comprehend— but we don't lead like He is. And for a portion of his life, David didn't either.

David's leadership was launched in God-honoring humility and dependence on the Lord for every concern. Then, as he rose in leadership ranks, garnering status, power, and financial reward, he loosened his connection to the One who chose him. Leaning on his position rather than the God who put him there for a purpose, David had to hit bottom before he could return to the level of trust in God that he had facing Goliath.

Our God-given opportunities to fight giants will be the most critical responsibilities God entrusts to us. How we respond to these tough challenges will define our leadership, our dependence on the Lord, and our ministry's future.

Never be afraid of giants because it is in these hardest trials that God gets all the credit. David told Saul and the army, ". . . everyone assembled here will know that the LORD rescues his people, but not

NEVER BE AFRAID OF GIANTS BECAUSE IT IS IN THESE HARDEST TRIALS THAT GOD GETS ALL THE CREDIT.

with sword and spear. This is the LORD's battle, and he will give you to us!" (1 Sam. 17:47).

As your ministry triumphs over giants, all will know that the honor and glory are God's alone. That is as good as it gets in ministry leadership.

Goliath never had a chance!

Notes

Chapter 3—The Big Idea—Sailboats Versus Powerboats

1. Roger Parrott, *The Longview: Lasting Strategies for Rising Leaders* (Colorado Springs: David C. Cook, 2009).

Chapter 4—Sea Legs or Seasickness

1. Rob Martin, *When Money Goes on Mission: Fundraising and Giving in the 21st Century* (Chicago: Moody Publishers, 2019).

Chapter 6—Leading Without a Plan Is the Plan

1. Donald Kraybill, *The Upside-Down Kingdom* (Harrisonburg, VA: Herald Press, 2018), 17.
2. Jim Collins, *Good to Great: Why Some Companies Make the Leap . . . and Others Don't* (New York: HarperBusiness, 2001), 22.
3. Ibid., 21.
4. Ibid., 27.
5. Jim Collins, "Level 5 Leadership," JimCollins.com, accessed July 2, 2021, https://www.jimcollins.com/concepts/level-five-leadership.html.
6. Lewis Carroll, *Alice's Adventures in Wonderland* (Project Gutenberg, 1991), chap. 6, https://www.gutenberg.org/files/11/11-h/11-h.htm.
7. Ralph Waldo Emerson, *Nature* (Boston: James Munroe & Company, 1849), 14.

Chapter 8—Making Decisions That Don't Just Solve the Problem

1. Roger Parrott, *The Longview: Lasting Strategies for Rising Leaders* (Colorado Springs: David C. Cook, 2009), 92–93.

2. Ibid.

Chapter 9—Getting Out in Front

1. Portions of this section were previously published in Roger Parrott, "Belhaven Football's Two Seasons – Story I Shared in Chapel," *Worldview Matters* (blog), August 28, 2012, http://blogs.belhaven.edu/president/2012/08/28/belhaven-footballs-two-seasons-story-i-shared-in-chapel/.

Chapter 10—Practicing Future-Focused Evaluation

1. "Anti-Semitism in the United States: General Grant's Infamy," Jewish Virtual Library, https://www.jewishvirtuallibrary.org/general-grant-s-infamy.
2. Roger Parrott, *The Longview: Lasting Strategies for Rising Leaders* (Colorado Springs: David C. Cook, 2009), 122.
3. Ron Chernow, *Grant* (New York: Penguin Press, 2017), 643.

Chapter 12—Embracing Speed

1. Christopher Harress, "The Sad End of Blockbuster Video: The One-time $5 Billion Is Being Liquidated as Competition from Online Giants Netflix and Hulu Prove All Too Much for the Iconic Brand," International Business Times, December 5, 2013, https://www.ibtimes.com/sad-end-blockbuster-video-onetime-5-billion-company-being-liquidated-competition-1496962.
2. Minda Zetlin, "Blockbuster Could Have Bought Netflix for $50 Million, but the CEO Thought It Was a Joke," *Inc.*, September 20, 2019, https://www.inc.com/minda-zetlin/netflix-blockbuster-meeting-marc-randolph-reed-hastings-john-antioco.html.
3. Marc Rudolph, *That Will Never Work: The Birth of Netflix and the Amazing Life of an Idea* (New York: Little, Brown and Company, 2019).
4. John H. Lienhard, "No. 1059: Inventing the Computer," *The Engines of Our Ingenuity*, https://www.uh.edu/engines/epi1059.htm.
5. "Movie Upturn: Attendance Is Gaining After Four-Year Drop, Theater Men Think They Say Better Pictures, War, TV's Tiresomeness Help," *The Wall Street Journal*, February 14, 1951: 1. ProQuest.

Chapter 13—Getting Comfortable with Risk

1. Quoted in Harvard Business Review, *Developing a Business Case: Expert Solutions to Everyday Challenges* (Boston: Harvard Business Review Press, 2010), 50.
2. Erica R. Hendry, "7 Epic Fails Brought to You by the Genius Mind of Thomas Edison," *Smithsonian*, November 20, 2013, https://www .smithsonianmag.com/innovation/7-epic-fails-brought-to-you-by-the-genius-mind-of-thomas-edison-180947786/.
3. "Elon Musk's Latest Rocket Launch Is a Successful Failure," *The Economist*, December 10, 2020, https://www.economist.com/science-and-technology/2020/12/10/elon-musks-latest-rocket-launch-is-a-successful-failure.

Chapter 14—Flexing for Implementation

1. Jim Collins, "First Who—Get the Right People on the Bus," JimCollins.com, accessed July 7, 2021, https://www.jimcollins.com/article_topics/articles/first-who.html.

Chapter 16—Realigning Focus

1. Andrew Thomas, "The Secret Ratio That Proves Why Customer Reviews Are So Important," *Inc.*, February 26, 2018, https://www .inc.com/andrew-thomas/the-hidden-ratio-that-could-make-or-break-your-company.html.
2. Alicia Kelso, "Business Lessons from the Late Founder of Chick-fil-A," September 8, 2014, QSRweb, https://www.qsrweb.com/articles/business-lessons-from-the-late-founder-of-chick-fil-a/.
3. Kristen McCabe, "51 Customer Review Statistics to Make You Rethink Using Them," Learn Hub, September 28, 2020, https://learn.g2.com/customer-reviews-statistics.

Chapter 18—I Never Planned . . .

1. The quotations in this chapter are from interviews with the author, November 2020 – February 2021.

"I encourage readers to embrace the thoughts contained in this valuable book."
Neil Nicoll, president and CEO of YMCA of the USA

the longview

the
longview
Lasting Strategies for Rising Leaders

Parrott
©

Roger Parrott, PhD

**Let's discuss
how Roger's
actionable insights
could trigger
transformation
for your ministry,
university, church,
or business.**

For media and speaking
inquiries contact
VoicesToConnect.com

Visit **OpportunityLeadership.com** to learn more.